PRICE
WITHDRAWN STOCK
FOR SALE
OXH

**Continuum** ***New Directions in Religion and Literature***

This series aims to showcase new work at the forefront of religion and literature through short studies written by leading and rising scholars in the field. Books will pursue a variety of theoretical approaches as they engage with writing from different religious and literary traditions. Collectively, the series will offer a timely critical intervention to the interdisciplinary crossover between religion and literature, speaking to wider contemporary interests and mapping out new directions for the field in the early twenty-first century.

*Blake. Wordsworth. Religion.* Jonathan Roberts

*Do the Gods Wear Capes?,* Ben Saunders

*England's Secular Scripture,* Jo Carruthers

*The New Atheist Novel*, Arthur Bradley and Andrew Tate

*Victorian Parables*, Susan E. Colón

**Forthcoming:**
*Glyph and the Gramophone*, Luke Ferretter

# THE LATE WALTER BENJAMIN

JOHN SCHAD

New Directions in Religion and Literature

continuum

**Continuum International Publishing Group**

The Tower Building
11 York Road
London SE1 7NX

80 Maiden Lane
Suite 704
New York NY 10038

www.continuumbooks.com



**British Library Cataloguing-in-Publication Data**
A catalogue record for this book is available from the British Library.

ISBN: HB: 978-1-4411-7170-2
PB: 978-1-4411-7768-1

**Library of Congress Cataloging-in-Publication Data**
Schad, John, 1960–
The late Walter Benjamin/John Schad.
p. cm. – (New directions in religion and literature)
Includes bibliographical references and index.
ISBN 978-1-4411-7768-1 (pbk.) –
ISBN 978-1-4411-7170-2 (hardcover)
1. Benjamin, Walter, 1892–1940–Fiction. 2. England–Fiction.
3. Experimental fiction. I. Title.

PR6119.C375L38 2012
823'.92–dc22
2011035571

Typeset by Deanta Global Publishing Services, Chennai, India
Printed and bound in India

For Lloyd Body

# CONTENTS

# PREFACE

You may, just possibly, be wondering what kind of book this is. Well, it may, I suppose, be most simply described as a kind of novel, in that it has a narrative of sorts and much of the action is fictional. To be more precise, though, it is a documentary novel in that, time and again, the narrative is being generated or informed by scraps of actual history – mostly newspaper clippings and personal testimonies. As you will see, these documentary fragments appear primarily as inserts within the narrative.

So, a documentary or 'found' novel, you might say – but I think it is still more a *readerly* novel, in that the action is driven not only by all these documentary texts but also by a central character who, whenever he speaks, only ever uses words gleaned verbatim from the voluminous writings of the German-Jewish intellectual Walter Benjamin (1892–1940). In this sense, my novel is one long act of reading – in particular of reading or re-reading the work and the life of Benjamin. The result, I hope, is that we see Benjamin not only askew but also afresh and in a manner that takes us a little closer to what his life and work might have meant or might yet come to mean.

This hope, of course, is no more or less than the kind of hope we find at the centre of much literary criticism, and *The Late Walter Benjamin* is, indeed, a kind of literary criticism; it is, though, criticism that is attempting to be itself literary – to be, if you will, a truly *literary* criticism. To put it another way, what follows is an act of reading or thinking that chooses to draw not upon the devices of argumentation that characterize most academic criticism, but instead upon the devices or strategies of literature, namely, plot, character, dialogue and so forth. We might call this, for want of better words, a 'critical-creative' work, a species of writing that I also attempt in my book, *Someone Called Derrida. An Oxford Mystery* (2007) and my co-edited book *Crrritic!* (2011).

I suspect this is more than enough by way of a preface, so please don't let me detain you any longer. However, should you want to know something about why or how the book came about, well, it began, I think, with a desire to consider some very particular words of Benjamin's – words written just months before he committed suicide in 1940. These words are 'every second [is]... the strait gate though which the Messiah might enter' and, as I began to think about them, I realized that the reason I found them so compelling is that, as a boy, I grew up within a church where talk of the Second Coming was sufficiently commonplace for the idea to play on my imagination. The result was that, as a boy, if I ever heard thunder at night, I felt drawn to the window to see if this was the moment in which Christ would return. In this sense, for my child-self, every second was indeed the strait gate through which the Messiah might enter.

This, then, is why I returned to the *time* of my childhood in the book that follows; but, as I did so, a second reason emerged, and this was the *place* in which I spent my childhood – a post-war council estate near London. For the more I thought about it, the more I felt that the estate was somehow pertinent to Benjamin's religious thinking, in particular the political and tragic-comic aspects of that thinking.

I should explain that I lived on the estate from 1965, aged 4, until 1982. We moved there from Swindon, following my father, who chose to go there to live and work as an evangelical minister of religion. What makes the estate so interesting vis-á-vis Walter Benjamin is that it sprang into existence, out of nothing as it were, in 1948 when 14,000 bombed-out Londoners were moved there. Once there, they found that they were living in a place, or no place, which the local press soon called 'a soulless wilderness' and likened to a 'Displaced Persons' Camp.' In a sense, then, I had on my hands the fact, or image, of a people in unbearable exile, even hell – an image of disaster that seemed to chime with the tragic notes within Benjamin's theology. At the same time, however, as my research developed, I was struck by the intense political self-consciousness of the estate that seemed to reflect the fact that it was planned and built in a spirit not only of national emergency but also of social utopianism – the estate was also known as the 'Promised Land' or 'Cockney Utopia.'

What follows is an attempt to freeze-frame this particular moment and, in doing so, to unleash, I hope, something of its politico-theological force. Important in this connection will, I think, be Benjamin's intense and peculiar engagement with a politicized Jewish theology, an engagement that issued, at the very end of his life, in what he called a 'weak Messianic force.' This was central to his complex, semi-mystical conviction that 'we' ourselves (an undefined revolutionary class or generation) should turn out to be, or have been, the Messiah that tarries, or indeed that might just 'enter' at 'every second.' Thus, the *Late Walter Benjamin* is an attempt to put this wild and ironic hope to the test of history, in particular the dangerous and largely unwritten history of the exiled working-class London that was post-war Oxhey.

To do this, very early on, I allow the action to slip from the mid 1960s of my childhood to the earliest days of the estate. To make this possible, I invent two stray and rather odd men, called Painter and Porlock, who seem to remember or indeed to live in the immediate post-war birth-moment of the estate. Painter seems to be a genuine working-class Londoner, whereas Porlock is probably not – he certainly does not speak like one, although he has somehow drifted onto the estate and has grown to convince himself that he belongs there.

The character that is a version of my 8-year-old self (the novel, in this sense, begins around 1968) is led into the world of Painter and Porlock after encountering an old man who seems to live with them. This old man says or thinks he is Walter Benjamin – or at last 'O. E. Tal,' one of several pseudonyms that Benjamin used. This figure, Mr Tal, is the character who only ever uses words actually written by Benjamin; each time he speaks is, then, a quotation, each one being referenced at the end of the book. Mr Tal, I should add, appears oblivious to the fact that the man with whom he is confused (Benjamin) has been dead for almost 30 years.

I hope you enjoy *The Late Walter Benjamin.*

> *Quotation. . . summons the word by its name, wrenches it destructively from its context, but precisely thereby calls it back to its origin.*
>
> *Walter Benjamin*

# ACKNOWLEDGEMENTS

As I guess you will have realized by now, this book is not only about Walter Benjamin but also the very early post-war days of a council estate just north of London called South Oxhey, the place where I grew up. My very first debt is, then, to all the past and present residents of the estate who kindly shared with me their memories of these days – namely: Maud Atkinson, Margaret Beech, Ray Breeze, Neil Hamilton, Don Jones, Joan Kennedy, John Laver, Joan Manning, June Moore, David Reidy, Alfred Rundle, Vanessa Sparrowhawk and Sorel Nunn.

The kindness of strangers is, of course, something to depend upon; witness the librarians and archivists who were also of tremendous help – particularly those at the British Library, the Hertfordshire Local Studies Library, the London Metropolitan Archives, Manchester Central Library, the People's History Museum in Manchester, South Oxhey Library and Watford Central Library.

Next to be named and unashamed are those who read and commented on early drafts of the book – namely, Katie Cohen, Roger Ebbatson, Ewan Fernie, Kevin Mills, Jonathan Taylor, Alice Vickers and John Vickers; and then there are those who, knowingly or not, encouraged or, in some way, assisted the project: namely, Anthony Grahame, Henry L. Carrigan Jr., Grelle White, Stephanie Hay, James Williams and indeed my mother, not to mention that 'nice man' (as she calls him) Ian McMillan who allowed me to read from the book on BBC Radio 3's *The Verb* back in January 2009.

An earlier version of the opening scenes appeared in Mark Knight (ed.), *Religion, Literature and Imagination* (London: Continuum, 2009). I am very grateful to them for permission to re-publish here.

At the last, thank you to Thomas, Bethan and Rebecca for not particularly caring if I am upstairs hiding in my so-called study. And then there is, there is, forever – Katie without whom, without whom, without whom....

# LIST OF ILLUSTRATIONS



The cover image and Figure 2.1 are reproduced by kind permission of the Israel Museum, Jerusalem. All Oxhey Estate images are from The South Oxhey Jubilee Calendar and are reproduced by kind permission of

Neil Hamilton on behalf of the Jubilee Committee. Figure 3.1 is reproduced by kind permission of the Three Rivers Museum and District Council (Rickmansworth). Figure 4.1 is reproduced by kind permission of Photo Gisèle Freund/IMEC/Fonds MCC. Figure 7.2 was kindly provided by Robert Fraser. Figure 8.1 is reproduced by kind permission of *The Daily Mirror.* Figure 12.1 is reproduced by kind permission of the Fundación Biblioteca Vitual Miguel de Cervantes, Miami University, Oxford, Ohio.

# LEFT BEHIND

You are about to encounter a man named Mr O. E. Tal, a man who lived in a place, a kind of settlement, called South Oxhey, a place near London that was built immediately after the World War II. It was, you see, built for bombed-out Londoners, working-class Londoners. Mr Tal, though, always claimed that he himself was a man from Berlin; in fact, he claimed that he was a dead man from Berlin, a very particular dead man, namely, Walter Benjamin, the German-Jewish intellectual. Walter Benjamin had died in 1940. To be precise, as I must, Benjamin committed suicide, and did so on September 26, 1940, in the Pyrenees, at the French-Spanish border, when his attempt to escape Nazi-occupied France appeared to have failed. He was, at that final hour, hoping to flee to America. However, he had, and this I shall stress, just a year before, considered making his first ever journey to England in order to seek asylum in London, along with his estranged wife, Dora, and their son, Stefan. In September 1939, both Dora and Stefan made it to London, and there they stayed and lived.

Little is known of their London lives, precious little. More, although not all, is known of the death of Walter Benjamin in the Pyrenees; and, of what is known, I cherish most the reports that he had with him a small case, or suitcase, in which, it is believed, he carried a manuscript that has since been lost, along with the case.

As you will see, O. E. Tal always carried a case, possibly in an attempt to fool the watchful world that he was, indeed, Walter Benjamin. Perhaps though, he, like so many, sought only to fool himself, and was successful in this deceit. Whatever, it was a very learned deception, since whenever Tal spoke, he employed only the written words of Walter Benjamin. And this he did with unswerving precision, as I can testify, having painstakingly checked and referenced each and every word.

Here, let me add that all the other quotations that appear in my text (from local newspapers, sociological surveys, passing poets and so forth) are also authentic, as are all the local voices that appear as inserts herein. Once or twice, the local voice is, I shall confess, my own, since for 17 years I lived, in a manner, on the estate, first as boy and then as alien. My father, you see, had taken us to South Oxhey to live; we moved there in 1965, from a railway town called Swindon. My father was a minister of religion and so went to South Oxhey to save souls. I no longer live there. I should have liked to stay but was blown away.

> *We who have died . . . are resurrected in what happens to us*
>
> *Walter Benjamin*

*South Oxhey LCC Estate*

**Figure 1.1** Oxhey Council Estate, c.1948

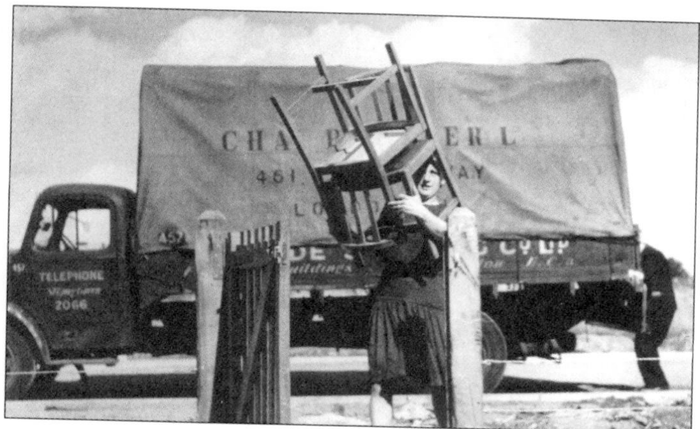


*"Moving In" – South Oxhey LCC Estate, 1949*

**Figure 1.2** Oxhey Council Estate, c.1948

*Totem Pole Road Signs*

**Figure 1.3** Oxhey Council Estate, c.1948

## SCENE ONE

# THE GATE

I could not have seen him coming, that clumsy man in the laughing shoes, he who merely stood there. Breathing and breathing. He was short and his jacket was like another's, one bigger than him, and his trousers were all terrible tight at the waist; but, after that, below that, they were like the trousers of Goliath. He carried a case, beaten up it was, and in his other hand he had until now, just now, gripped a paper shopping bag, brown and old as forever. At last, on his forehead, sweat glistered like a well-made curse. As for his hair, a wild game, it was as ash.

At first, I thought the clumsy man was one of the mad, the-mad-with-anger, as if someone, say, a boy, such as I, had thrown a ball into his garden. But then, I reasoned that here, before me, stood a man who had, quite simply, seen enough and was weary, what with his crumbling face pulled right down to those laughing shoes, by spectacles all heavy and round, and a moustache, black as a piano.

He finally spoke, this man in the shoes, saying he was called 'Tal' – T-A-L, Tal. Mr Tal. It was an unlikely name, I thought, as was his voice, half-German, half-lost. That of a Jew.

For a moment, this Mr Tal returned to silence, but then he spoke again, slowly, as if reading from a book. 'For the Jews' (he breathed) 'every second of time' (he breathed) 'was the strait gate through which' (he breathed) 'the Messiah might enter.'

I nodded and said I'd be fleeing, but his bag sat weeping on the ground between us, the shopping bag he'd dropped and that had spilled its guts just as we were about to cross. The moment it had hit the ground, I'd offered to help him, imagining myself the Good Samaritan and he the man bound for Jericho. But I don't think Mr Tal heard me, for he simply bent low over his bag and its guts and said, 'I am unpacking my library.'

> *West Herts and Watford Observer*
> June 29, 1951
> Whatever happened to the Promised Land? 14,000 bombed-out London workers and their families have been uprooted to rural Hertfordshire, plunged into a Wilderness, and left to their own devices. So says an official Hertfordshire County Council report. According to the report, the Oxhey Estate has proved a monstrous misconception of re-housing, a spectacular failure on the part of The London County Council to create the promised land of Cockney Utopia.

Mr Tal had, by now, packed up his library, returned it to his shopping bag and was ready to fly; but, seeing how he struggled with it all, again I vowed to help. The clumsy man said nothing, and so I followed him with his heavy friend in my arms. Mr Tal held on to his beaten leather case, square and black, neither quite suitcase nor briefcase. It was clear that he thought the world of this case, guarding it with his life as if it were, you might say, the Ark of the Covenant. And so, on we promenaded, all along my road, the two of us, myself with his bag and he with the Ark. Soon, others were staring: three deadly thieves, a dog that smiled and two coughing saints who tended to a dying car.

Mr Tal shuffled along. And, strange to say, all the time, he kept to the right. 'These Londoners,' he explained, 'their only agreement is that everyone should keep to the right of the pavement.' His head was bent as if he were looking for his shoes, his body at 11 o'clock. Although the way was flat, he alone ascended a mountain.

As we moved, I thought of how the houses were the same and how they all were bordered by the same species of hedge, except one that had no hedge, no hedge at all. Mr Tal slowed as he approached the house without hedge, although it did boast a gate, a solitary gate that stood alone, as if a tooth, alone.

The old man seemed to live in this house, and so I thought he would eschew the gate, just as the world did. To reach the front door, all he need do was cut across the grass, but this was not his way; instead, he limped right on up to the tooth. And, once there, at the very tooth, he stopped and half turned about, a slow pirouette. He now faced the house. Face to face. Still, very still. It was as if Mr Tal always did this, as if he forever made a point and a show of stopping at the gate. Hesitation, a ritual. Then off he stumbled, up along the garden path and towards the pale front door. It was somewhere between green and grey, and stood open to all. Once there, Mr Tal coughed, ready to speak. 'The solution to the riddle of the universe,' he whispered, 'is to be found where we would least expect it.'

*West Herts and Watford Observer*
July 6, 1951

Dear Sir,

For any person non-resident on our estate to read your article, a sordid mental picture is aroused, ranging in verbal hue from the squalor of an eastern native quarter to an isolated and forgotten Displaced Persons camp. Unfortunately, for some, council estates still have the ring of drab green-and-brown walls, coals in the bath and a mild flavour of Public Assistance.

Yours sincerely,
Mr D.F. Haydon
(110 Prestwick Road)

Mr Tal stared at the open door, but was unable to move. 'I am standing on the threshold about to enter,' he said. 'It is a complicated business,' he added.

'It *is*?' I responded.

'I must,' he explained, 'make sure of landing on a plank travelling at twenty miles a second round the sun and the plank has no solidity of substance.' He looked quite anxious. 'To step on it shall I not slip through?'

'I don't think so,' I said.

Mr Tal considered for a while, and straightened his tie. It was blackened, utterly. He thought a little more, and straightened his tie again. He then pulled up Goliath's trousers and careered head first through a window, open wide to the spinning world. His case had pursued him and, for a moment, all I could see of Mr Tal were the gleaming soles of his shoes. Soon, his head appeared at the window and he waved at me. Should I follow? I was not sure, but on I went, though beginning to lose the struggle with his library. By now a bagful of sand.

*West Herts and Watford Observer*
July 27, 1951

Dear Sir,
I came to Oxhey from Fulham and curse the day we moved here . . . Say one word and the language from even the youngest child would not bear printing. The only time we get any peace is when it is pouring

with rain. The East End is quiet and respectable compared to this.
Yours sincerely,
Mrs H.H.
(full name withheld)

The room into which I had landed knew no carpet, and someone, I thought, must have run away with at least half the furniture. All that remained was an ample settee, three hard-backed chairs and a high wooden table. Sadly, a cripple. On the table sat an ashtray, and on the ashtray leaned a lit cigarette, coolly smoking itself. Someone, I thought, had just left the room, someone who had been eyeing the television in the corner. It was an ancient television, a stout Bakelite set that simply stood there, complacent, like a miracle. And on it, on its Bakelite top, stood a snow globe, a tiny glass snow globe.

Mr Tal set down his case, looked around and almost smiled. 'Knickknacks, knickknacks everywhere,' he said, 'feather duster, hairdryer and Venus de Milo, champagne bottles, prostheses, and letter-writing manuals.' He almost smiled again.

I could see only the feather duster and the hairdryer, but said nothing, my mind being bent on the television set, busily leaking light entertainment into the abandoned room. And I watched as a wisecracking comedian staggered to the punchline of the wisest crack of all. But this seemed to anger Mr Tal and, with automatic hand, he condemned the comedian to oblivion. 'The electronic television,' he muttered. He had switched it off at the very moment the comedian was to bring down the house. Now, all I could see was his wisecracking face grow smaller and smaller until a tiny white dot.

I stared at the dot as it vanished, and grieved. But Mr Tal did not mourn, he simply waved his arms and spoke. 'The arrangement of the furniture,' he declared, 'is the site plan of deadly traps and prescribes the fleeing victim's path.' Then, right then, something thin and light moved in the hallway and someone, a young woman, I think, stole past yet another open door. She ran up a staircase, bare and sharp.

'Who's that?' I asked.

'The whore called "Once upon a time,"' he said.

'Oh I see,' I said.

'The fleeing victim,' he added.

'Oh I see,' I said.

I believed if I stared very hard at where the white dot had been that the television might yet come to its senses, and when Mr Tal shuffled towards it I could not help but hope, hope against hope. Instead, though, of reaching for the set itself he simply picked up the tiny glass snow globe and gave it a terrible shake. For a moment, its miniature house disappeared in a miniature blizzard. 'Science,' he sighed, 'sees in atoms nothing but electron storms.'

Yes, a physicist, I thought, as he then put the house back on the set just to the left of where he had found it. 'The Messiah,' he remarked, 'did not wish to change the world by force, but only to make –' (he paused) '– a slight adjustment in it.'

A holy man, I thought. Much like my father.

*West Herts and Watford Observer*
July 6, 1951

Following the heated debate triggered by the County report on the Oxhey estate, we sent a reporter to knock on the door of some of the folk that live there. Here's what Mrs J. Nielson of 15 Muirfield Road had to say: 'Am I happy? Well, I think it's what people make of it, don't you? They can either make it a heaven . . . or something else.'

Mr Tal looked back to the window whence he had made his entry, and muttered. 'In the re-purified Garden of Eden,' he said, 'nothing remains but the question whether it is paradise or hell.'

'Yes,' I said.

I was now ready to go in search of my home and whoever might still be there, but Mr Tal had seized his case and waved his empty hand at a door to another room. It was smaller than the first, and here somebody, I thought, must have vanished along with yet more of the furniture. Left behind was an upturned packing case, a trembling tower of books and papers, a paraffin heater that smelled to high heaven, a radiogram almost the size of a coffin and two very stiff wooden chairs. Here were dumped two men sleeping. Furiously.

One was a tumbled giant ensnared in a heavy double-breasted overcoat. Beneath the coat, I could see a collar and a tie that longed to strangle the giant. Here, I thought, is a man in readiness. He was a little younger than Mr Tal, although this titan's face was hard as if he'd been taken outside and punched forever. Rock of Ages, I thought; unlike the fellow with him, who was just as tall but thinner and younger and dressed up in a brown three-piece suit that was fast fading away. This thinner, younger man wore shining brown shoes, though they had no laces. Both men spread their legs and arms all over the place and looked, I thought, quite astonished. Marionettes, a pair of murdered marionettes, I thought.

Mr Tal pointed his case at the sleeping men. 'There is no telling,' he said, 'what encounters would be in store for us if we were less inclined to give in to sleep.' He then gave each sleeper a mortal kick upon the shins. 'The angel,' he said, 'would like to awaken the dead.'

The dead, I could see, didn't like being awoken, not even by an angel. In fact, for an instant, they looked like two who had been newly accused. But this passed, blew over and it was clear they were mad, hopping mad, hopping bloody mad.

'You're late!' they cried. At first, I thought the dead spoke to *me*, but it was Mr Tal they addressed.

'And the food?' said the giant, jumping to his feet. He was called Painter, Victor Painter.

Mr Tal stared nothing.

'Liver and prunes –,' interjected the thin man, who added, for my benefit, that he was Dr E. Porlock, E-for-Earnest Porlock.

'Liverandprunes,' he resumed, 'liverandprunes, liverandprunes, liverandprunes. And, please God, no more of your damnable books.' He remained on his chair, although now cross-legged.

I was about to say I knew nothing of any liverandprunes when Mr Tal shook his head.

'No, no more of my damnable books,' said his head.

'About time,' said Porlock, whose face was like a second-hand face, a hand-me-down face. He had, though, the voice of a drunken lord; well spoken but loose, worn, arch, knowing, fallen. Porlock smoothed his hair. It receded. He smoothed it again. 'His room,' he said, gesturing towards Mr Tal, 'is already an ocean of books.' Mr Tal nodded. 'One of the most remarkable reading rooms in the world,' he whispered to himself.

**Figure** 1.4 Oxhey Estates United, 1952.

Back Row. First left: V. Painter.* Far right: The Rent-Man.*, Front row. Second right: E. Porlock.*

## SCENE TWO

# THE HOUSE

I sat on the radiogram, looking all about me. Nothing. Silence crowded the room. And through the silence I whispered how my father ran the church across the road. The room did not respond. 'The church opposite.' Still nothing from the room. 'The one with the cross that lights up.' Nothing again. 'And there's this big glass,' I said, 'that's left in the pulpit each Sunday, left with water in it, water for the preacher.' Nothing nothing. 'And the funny thing,' I said, 'is that on this glass you can see that it says – ' (nothing nothing nothing) '– you can see that it says, "This glass has been stolen from The Dick Whittington Public House."'

> 'Yes, there was some petty crime, but, then, the LCC hadn't moved fourteen-thousand angels straight from heaven to the estate. . . . '

'Turn again, turn again,' said Painter, rising, and beginning to walk the room, 'Turn again, again and again.' He paused. 'Bloody Promised Land,' he said.

*Estate News*

Vol. 1, August 1949

> When we arrived we were very much strangers in a strange land. (Editor)

'Jacked it in, they have. Hundreds. All pissing off back to London. They take one look at this place and say,

"There's bugger-all here." And you know what?' He stared in my direction.

I said 'No.'

'Well, they're *right*, that's what,' he said, 'No pubs, no shops, no jobs. No nothing. NonothingNonothingNo-nothing.' He stopped and stared from the window.

*Hertfordshire County Council / Education Committee, 1951*

> After three years we regret to say that, apart from one small café, the Oxhey estate would appear to have no public amenities whatever.

'No pavement,' added Painter, 'no bloody pavement.'

Porlock produced a cigarette and observed that there weren't any *roads* as yet and thus the lack of pavement was, on the whole, and, all things considered, neither Here nor There.

Painter paused and then spoke, again his words huddled together. 'Mudandduckboards,' he said, 'mudandduckboards, mudandduckboards, mudandbloodyduckboards.'

'Not unlike the Somme,' said Porlock. He smiled. And as he smiled, Mr Tal lifted his case, balanced it atop that tower of books and papers, then opened his case and busily went through it.

Pause.

'*And so* –,' said Porlock, as he turned to me, '– welcome to Nowhere, Nowhere near London; or, to be more precise, Nowhere near Watford, which is to say Nowhere near Nowhere.'

'But who,' said Painter, 'who the hell can afford the bus?' He was walking the room again.

'The bus?'

'The bus to bloody Watford.'

Porlock, still seated, pointed out that there *weren't* any buses, none whatsoever. He felt that, all in all, this helped matters. Painter did not feel this.

'The man from the Council,' said Painter, 'he says, "Put on your hat and be happy, Mr. Painter; things will improve. It may," he says, "take a thousand years to build the New Jerusalem, and a little longer to get a bus to Watford, BUT, my friend, be grateful you have anywhere. Besides," he says, "out here you have woods and fields. Just look," he says, "just look at the lovely trees, the lovely trees. . . ." "But what," I says, "is the use of all these bloody trees? There are only so many of the buggers cos there's nothing else."'

'Be careful,' said Porlock, 'trees have ears.' He struck a match. It flamed.

> '. . . It was so quiet, so very quiet. . . The Hertfordshire folk may have liked their country walks. . . but to most of us it was just empty space. We felt so alone and stranded out here. . . .'

'Trees,' murmured Painter, still walking, 'What *is* the bloody point?'

'Firewood,' replied Porlock, lighting up. 'These trees are here for us to burn in our otherwise empty grates. Consider them a gift. From a grateful nation.' He flung the match at the paraffin heater, and missed.

'Grateful for what?' I asked, from the radiogram.

'Why, for disappearing,' said Porlock, 'for hiding out here, where no one can see us, no can see us shiver, so cold as it is and so sick as we are.'

'Sick?'

'Ah, did you not know? Have you not heard?' said Porlock. He began to smoke. 'This here is Tubercular-Town, The Sanatorium in the Woods.' He smiled. 'Hence myself, Dr. Porlock.' He crossed his thin, fragile legs, and inhaled.

> Because so many of the families who were moved to the estate had health problems, there were, in the early days, ceaseless Public Health studies, most involving incredibly detailed questionnaires of up to forty questions.

Porlock lifted an eyebrow and tasted a little more smoke. He then announced that 'Once upon a time' ('Just last bloody month,' said Painter) he, Dr. Porlock, had been 'in the way of wandering the estate asking benign and tender folk benign and tender questions such as –'

'Do you have trouble passing water?' said Painter.

'I beg your pardon,' said Porlock, from his chair.

'Do you have trouble passing water?' said Painter, 'You knocked and said, "Do you have trouble passing water?"'

'No, just the pub,' said Porlock.

Pause.

Mr Tal looked up from his case. 'The touring medical expert,' he said, 'conquered this statistical Matterhorn.' He pointed at the estate.

'Not merely,' said Porlock, 'the Matterhorn.' He flicked at some dandruff that lay on his shoulder. 'There was also . . . .' He appeared to be about to make his confession.

'We know,' said Painter, walking aroundandaround. 'We know we know we know,' said Painter.

'In that case,' said Porlock, 'I shall fall silent, irresistibly silent. Suffice it to say, though, the whole sorry episode goes some way to explaining why the hell I seem to be here.' He pointed to the paraffin heater, but I think he meant the house.

Painter suddenly stopped, right beside me. 'Dr. Pillock here,' he said, 'now thinks he's one of us.'

'The sickening surgeon,' said Porlock, touching an invisible hat. 'Pleased as man with man to dwell – even sick man. Even,' (he paused), 'those whom we must call "tubercular persons."' He coughed.

I felt for the collar of my shirt, as I had been taught to do in the playground whenever an ambulance went past. A cockney rite, I have since learnt.

Mr Tal looked up once again from his case. 'Illness here,' he whispered, 'is a social emblem.'

'Exactly,' said Porlock. 'Read to him, Painter.'

Porlock, still cross-legged, reached inside his jacket and pulled out a thin set of papers. He handed one to Painter, who, finally coming to a standstill, did exactly as bidden. '"General Practice on a New Housing Estate,"' read Painter, 'By J.H.F. Brotherstone and S.P.W. Chave (London School of Health and Tropical Medicine).'

'*Topical*,' said Porlock, '*Topical* Medicine.' Through smoke.

'*With*,' went on Painter, 'A. Clewyn-Davies, A.S. Hunter, D.A. Lindsay, A. Scott, C.B. Thomas and – ' (he paused) '– E.J. Trimmer.'

'E.J. Trimmer?' said Porlock.

Painter waved his hand and carried on: '"Forty-five per cent of the families on the estate have –' (he slumped towards the floor) '– have been re-housed on medical grounds."'

'You see!' said Porlock, addressing Mr Tal. He then turned to Painter and, holding out another slip of paper, compelled him once more to read.

Painter was upon the floor, his back to the wall, but again he did as ordered. '*The Milbank Memorial Fund Quarterly*, vol. 37. no. 4 (1959),' he read. Slowly, he read.

'Time –,' whispered Porlock, '– remember the time.'

Painter remembered, and quickened: 'Backache. Catarrh. Depression. Eyestrain. Headaches.'

'Nothing for F'?

'No, no Flatulence.'

'Headaches. Indigestion. Nerves. Personality Disorders. *Running Ears.*' Painter stopped at 'Running Ears.' Porlock said he had never seen any. Painter pressed on.

'Sleeplessness. Stomach Pains. Swollen Ankles. *Teeth.*'

'Teeth?'

'Yes.'

'*Just* "Teeth"?'

'Yes.'

'Disappointing.'

'Undue Irritability. Varicose Veins. Weak or Painful Feet . . . and –' (Painter paused) ' . . . *Women's Complaints.*'

Porlock, unmoved from his chair, fumbled at a joke, a gag, a crack, a funny, one that juggled women, complaints and himself. But it all fell about him. Painter winced, and that girl, the one I had seen before, stared from the open door, just for a second. She must have fallen quietly down the stairs, and now looked, for all the world, as if about to speak.

'Summoned or un-summoned, the secretary enters,' said Mr Tal, from his post at the tower of books and papers. 'She is,' he added, 'very pretty.'

Nothing.

Porlock was still thinking of the Sick, and the questions they had been asked, and those who had not answered, the report being called 'The Families and Individuals Who Did Not Co-Operate on a Sample Survey.' 'It was,' said Porlock, 'a survey of those who refuse to answer surveys'. Pause. 'Such as Painter,' he said. 'Or the Jew. Not one for surveys, is the Jew.'

'At midnight,' murmured Mr Tal, 'a questionnaire on the death penalty is distributed to the cells requiring its signatories to indicate which form of execution they would prefer.'

Painter was now, it seemed, condemned to read again, his eyes hobbling on, word after word, and this time his gaze landed, heavy, upon, '"The person who refuses to answer questions, or sometimes even to *come to the door*."'

'That'll be Herr Tal,' said Porlock. 'He has trouble with doors.'

'No,' said Painter, 'Tal's the next one, *this* one.' Painter read aloud the sad case of a weary man, a weary 'Non Co-operator,' who had, one day, lifted his weary head and wearily cried, 'Why are people always worrying me?' The weary man had then, apparently, said this: 'I have just about had it, what with Jehovah's Witnesses and all the rest.'

'The weary man,' said Porlock, 'has, as ever, a point. One day a man is at my door wanting to know if I have constipation, the next he pops round to let me know that the world will end Tuesday next. Tell that to the man from Social Medicine.'

'I *did*,' said Painter, without looking up from his place by the wall.

'And what happened?' asked Porlock.

'He moved in, the bastard,' said Painter.

Pause.

Painter was ready to read again, his head still full of Non Co-operators. 'Listen,' he said, 'Listen to this: "Those who gave only one interview might be reluctant to be interviewed again lest it be discovered"' (Painter coughed) '"lest it be discovered that they now lived here"' (he coughed again) '"on false pretences, because"' (he paused) '"because *they were no longer ill*."'

'Or,' said Porlock, 'no longer *dead*.' He stared at his shoes, he admired them. Although laceless, they were certainly identical.

'I'm sorry?' I said.

Porlock had no answer to my question. But Mr Tal did. 'Even the dead,' he said, 'will not be safe from the enemy if he wins.'

Porlock said he wondered quite how much Herr Tal knew of the dead, particularly when compared to, say, Mr Painter. 'Of the dead,' added Porlock, 'Mr V. Painter knows more than ever he might betray.'

Mr Tal nodded. 'Was it not noticeable,' he asked, 'at the end of the war that men returned from the battlefield grown silent?'

'Yes, yes it was,' I said, interrupting the world, from upon the radiogram. I said that, in fact, I knew, down the road, a flattened old man who had been rung through the mangle of Flanders. One day the flattened man, I said, had given me a crucifix made of bullet shells, shells collected from the beach at Ypres, but had whispered nothing of the beach or the mangle.

'Enough,' said Porlock.

But on I ploughed, on to how, a little later, the flattened man had tried to hang himself. Everyone knew. And how, soon after, at a Christmas party held in the church, I had spied him sat at a table and eating red jelly and opening his cracker and finding within both a paper-crown and a tiny plastic pistol. He had turned to his wife, I said, his crown lopsided, and pointed the toy gun to the side of his royal head and smiled. But he did not speak, I said. His wife, though, *did* break the silence, saying he should return to the bloody jelly.

Quiet.

Painter rose, slowly, to his feet, and lifted high the inverted packing case. There, right there, stood a huge reel-to-reel cine projector. As Painter began to animate its parts, Mr Tal grew still, by the tower. He breathed and the tower trembled. He was thinking, it seemed, about the man with the paper-crown. 'In a dream,' said Mr Tal, 'I took my life with a gun. When it went off

I did not wake up but saw myself lying. Only then did I wake.'

'Waking,' said Porlock, 'is invariably an error.' He coughed into his handkerchief. 'Out here we know better – we, the exported dead of London.' He smiled. 'They say we are not fourteen-thousands angels, but just look at us. Look at us.' He pointed to the evidence.

'The angel,' said Mr Tal, trying to help, 'the angel of history.'

'What?' said Painter. He looked up from the projector.

'The angel of history,' said Mr Tal, 'the angel would like to stay but a storm is blowing from Paradise.'

'Bugger the angel,' murmured Painter.

'To quote the men of Sodom,' said Porlock.

Painter returned to his projector, and Porlock spoke of 'passing the time.'

*West Herts and Watford Observer*
November 21, 1952

> Mr and Mrs Alfred Nutt, residents on the Oxhey estate, have made enough toys to fill a complete stall for the Clitheroe Club sale of work. Mr Nutt, a woodworker, has made three ducks, three railway engines, two trucks, a boat on wheels, and half a dozen monkeys on a stick. Mrs Nutt has made over twenty stuffed toys. When asked how they came to make so much, Mr Nutt explained, 'It gives us something to do. You see, we have all day.'

Mr Tal nodded, as if he agreed with someone. 'This storm,' he said, 'propels the angel of history into the future.'

'Storm?' said the projectionist.

Mr Tal nodded.

'The one that blows from Paradise?' said Porlock.

Mr Tal nodded.

'Shit!' said the projectionist.

Mr Tal nodded yet again and remarked that, 'This storm is what we call Progress.'

'*Dispersal*,' said Painter.

Mr Tal was at sea.

'Ship-the-bloody-workers-out,' said Painter, '– *Dispersal*. Here they call it *Dispersal*.'

'The Export of Populace,' said Porlock.

'Overspill,' said Painter.

'Spontaneous –,' said Porlock, '– Spontaneous Mass Decentralisation.'

'Storm,' said Mr Tal, now seeming to understand, 'Storm from paradise.'

Then the girl, that girl, appeared once more, and we tumbled into silence. This time, she looked in at us through a sudden window and from a sudden garden, new, so new. Hardly a garden, I thought. The girl wore terrible lipstick and stared at the three men and myself, God's little historian. I thought I could hear the girl think.

War or weather, she wondered, which is it? Which is the reason, the reason we are here? Is it true we were born, stillborn, in a storm? And is that why we only get peace when it pours? When it storms.

*West Herts and Watford Observer*
April 8, 1949

A small worker's canteen on the Oxhey estate was, on Thursday, the birthplace of a Community Association. The hut was crammed to capacity with over 300 residents and, in darkness relieved only by the flickering light of two hurricane lamps, this pioneer movement was born.

'Little Moscow,' said Painter.

'Pardon?' said Porlock.

'They call us Little Moscow,' said Painter.

'Quite,' said Porlock.

'Ask for a clinic,' said Painter, 'and you're bloody Stalin.'

'Who?' said Porlock.

Pause.

Painter had now something else to read, to read aloud; although this time it had emerged as if from his flesh, from deep inside his coat. '*The Advancement of Science*,' he muttered. '1956,' he muttered. '"Social and Psychological Aspects of Re-Housing," he muttered. 'H.G. Maule,' he concluded.

I longed to stay, to stay awake, to know, to learn, to heed whatever it was that H.G. Maule had written. And so I stayed.

'"It was,"' read Painter, '"in the very early days that the Community Association began its *Agitation.*"' He stopped at 'Agitation.' Then on he trudged: '"And back then its motives were widely regarded as being . . . "' (he was mired again) '". . . as being *Political.*"'

'There!' said Painter. He hurled *The Advancement* way over his shoulder. But Porlock, for a moment abandoning his chair, rescued *The Advancement*. Then, sitting down again, he read aloud the next sentence as if he himself were H.G. Maule: '"While, though, I do believe there were political motivations,"' mimicked Porlock, '"I should not want to underestimate the tendency of such situations to bring to the fore certain . . . *rather aggressive types of personality.*"'

Porlock glared at Painter who bellowed to God, crumpled in an almighty heap and clutched his caryatid head.

'What it is,' whispered Porlock, 'to find that someone out there really does know you.' He too now hurled *The Advancement of Science* as far as he could.

Painter got up, slow as the earth, and bent, again, to his projector. 'Dear machine,' he whispered.

Porlock stooped down and drew from beneath his chair a pure white book. On the front ran the words, 'County of London Plan, 1943.' He crossed his legs once more, thin-thin-thin, and held the book upside down.

Mr Tal closed his case, left the trembling tower, moved to the window and stared into the garden; it was the girl again, the motherless girl. She was looking up at the sky, her hands in the pockets of a knee-length skirt that was of faraway blue. She wore short socks that were white like surrender, and shoes that were pointed. Next to her, I could see a transistor radio, and soon she was swaying to an electrified song. Outside, I thought, the empty air must at last be full, full of America.

When Mr Tal grew conscious that I too observed the girl, he spoke, saying, ever so slowly, 'I have met a woman here who is the female counterpart of the Angelus Novus.'

Mr Tal then dragged from within his jacket a sorry postcard. Fragile. As if glass. The old man beckoned to me. I jumped from the wireless, flitted across the room and eyed the card, my mouth agape, and saw a figure, hardly human, with clumsy arms, or wings. Raised in holy defeat. Its eyes were wide and alarmed and looked to the side. I thought it smiled.

'A painting,' said Mr Tal, 'named Angelus Novus.' He straightened his blackened tie. 'Angelus Novus,' he said, 'an angel looking as though he is about to move away from something he is fixedly contemplating. His eyes are staring, his mouth is open, his wings are spread.'

'Angel?' I said. Mr Tal peered once more from the window. 'I have met here,' he whispered, 'the *female* Angelus Novus.'

'And is she pretty?' I said, 'Is she pretty?'

Mr Tal turned his head and whispered again. 'The only person,' he began, 'the only person I intend to introduce as a neophyte to this angelology. . . .'

'Is who?' I asked.

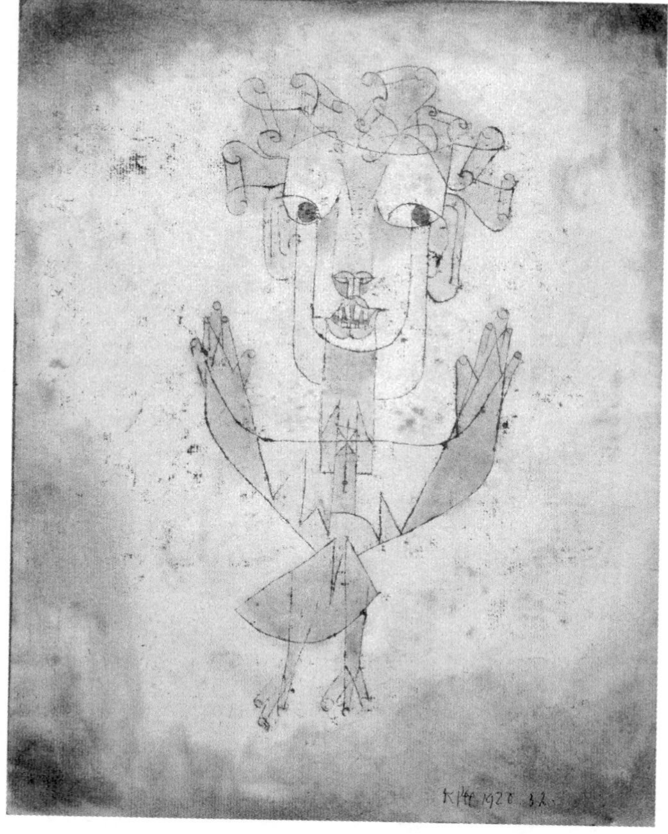

**Figure 2.1** Paul Klee, *Angelus Novus*, (1920)

'The only person . . . ,' he began again.

'Is *who*?' I said again. 'Is *who*?'

Nothing, he said nothing, even as I looked out at the girl, who was, by now, tightrope walking along a washing line that had fallen, naked, to the grass. I was about to whisper to the girl, but was overcome by the whirr-whirr-whirr of Painter's tragic projector – his 'Light of the World,' he said, as if to curse it. He then pulled the curtains, and the girl disappeared. Angela Nova.

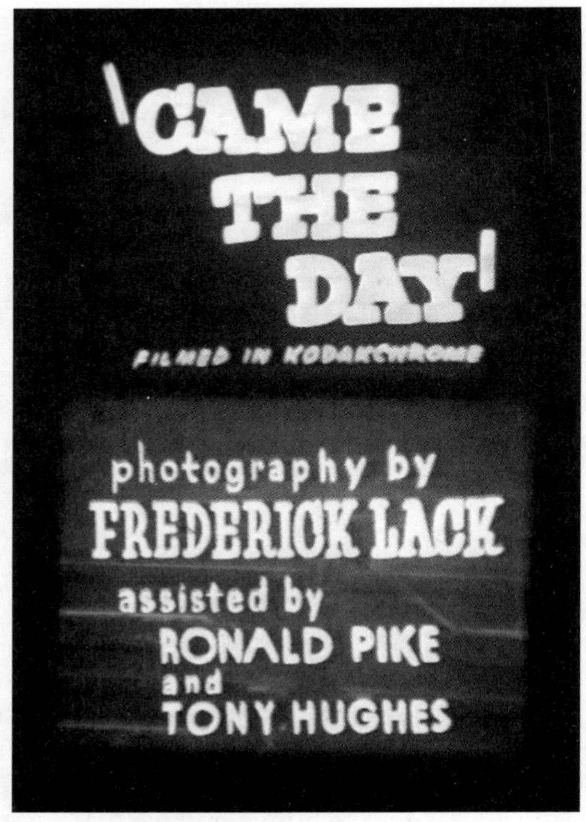


**Figure 3.1** 'Came the Day,' 1957, film of South Oxhey Carnival

## SCENE THREE

# TWO FILMS ARE BRIEFLY PROJECTED

Mr Tal, now seated on a chair, stared at the wall, expectant. On one side of him stood his case, on the other side I stood as if a footman. Like Mr Tal, I stared and expected. The wall, our screen, madly papered, as if in a fit, blinked for an instant in the light. The words, 'Came the Day,' then flickered into focus. The opening frame. It had little colour, this frame, but it promised that the world to-come would be in 'Kodakchrome.' This was a world made of luminous, daydream colour, like something or someone from, say, America.

> In 1957 the Oxhey Estate Community Association produced a twenty-minute film of the estate carnival, a huge affair that seems to have mobilised almost everyone. The film is beautifully crafted and begins with shots of the estate filmed from a plane.

It is dawn, and a pale figure is stooping to lift from the pavement a single piece of paper. The pale figure then runs his finger along words that announce the Coming Day. CARNIVAL, it says, CARNIVAL. And the word is also there on a banner pulled by a plane across a sky that is empty and drawn by a child. There is some kind of music, but it is broken by the most terrible breathing. The cinematographer is tubercular.

On the wall, I can see that the pale man with the piece of paper is a dustman. He and his finger have now done reading, and the film spins back in time to the days before

The Day That Came. I must have been watching, I reason, the Day That Came After.

Mr Tal is still staring at the wall, but it is as if he is seeing the film a few seconds late. 'What we will see,' he says, 'is a rag-picker, at daybreak, picking up rags of speech.' Pause. 'A rag-picker early on, at the dawn of the day of the revolution.'

Porlock, head bowed, is still staring at his inverted book, but he asks that someone tell Mr Tal that revolutions are not to be mistaken for carnivals. 'Revolutions,' he adds, 'entail less loss of life.'

Mr Tal says nothing as the film wheels on and the roads of Utopia are made to sway by American marching-bands that are cheered and followed by hundreds of Utopians, most on foot and some on bikes. The tenants of Nowhere are storming a beautiful future. Their roads are now streets and they are a crowd again.

But I see, out of the hole in my eye, that two people, just two people, are hurtling the opposite way, towards the back of the crowd. One is a worried woman, her head in a shopping bag, and the other is a tramp on a bike. He looks, I think, like Mr Tal, who remarks, with a sigh, that 'The quest for happiness runs *counter* to the Messianic direction.' He then adds, 'I had quietly turned my back on the carnival and strolled down to the harbour.'

'Harbour?' said Porlock, still not looking up. He suspected that Mr Tal was busy watching quite the wrong film.

The right film then crashed, without a word, as a mother stood at a gate, waving farewell to a daughter who was bound for the Carnival. The mother had applied a final line of lipstick, but now she too is gone. She is gone, the mother. The great projector had failed.

Painter walloped the machine, his history machine. 'Buggered,' he said.

'Like a cuckold,' said Porlock.

Painter pulled off one monstrous reel and threw on another. The second film was so very old as to bleed in black-and-white and never to have learnt to talk.

This time, in this film, we who watch, Mr Tal and I, are strangers on a train, a steam train, and we, along with the camera, are battered by a landscape that hurtles the other way, a fleeing world of whirling trees and fields. Soon, though, the fields and trees begin, one by one, to come to their senses, as we descend into an infinite city. Then, of a sudden, the city has a name, as both train and camera steam towards a sign that whispers 'BERLIN.'

> *Berlin: Symphony of a Great City*, a 1927 avant-garde German silent film directed by Walter Ruttmann, portrays the life of a city, mainly through visual impressions in a semi-documentary style. The events of the film are arranged to simulate the passage of a single day. Shots and scenes are cut together based on relationships of image, motion, point of view, and thematic content. Much of Walter Benjamin's writings about Berlin are thought to parallel Ruttman's film and others that are like it. Ruttmann's film was popular in England and, as it happens, was screened by the Watford Film Society on February 16, 1951.

By now, our train-to-Berlin has come to a theatrical halt, and we are looking down long and hollow streets. Berlin. Once again, it is dawn, the world has not quite yet begun, and no one is here, not a soul. Berlin. The first I see has a painted, man-made face and wears a chemise that reveals bare and beautiful shoulders. This frozen Eve is a mannequin and stands in a window. Berlin. After a while, an Adam appears, a man with a dog who thinks upon the pavement; and soon others emerge to set the streets on edge. Berlin. First, empty-handed workers walk defence-less to the factory; then, men of business steal towards the office on trams; at last, leisured men and ensnared women, divine automata, waltz through the arcades of a city half in love with itself. Berlin.

And, all the while, Mr Tal, still seated, case beside him, is watching with a most peculiar passion, like a man seeing death for the very last time. Berlin. 'People,' says Mr Tal, 'are taught to cry again by films.' Berlin. Berlin.

Mr Tal now rose to his feet and tugged at a pipe that stood, head first, inside his ill-fitting jacket. He wielded the pipe as if it were a piece of himself, a piece I thought he was just about to set aflame until he gripped the pipe in a fist that was clenched and, with it, declared war on Painter's projector. In no time, none at all, he had quite poked out the once bright eye of the glaring Cyclops. The show was over.

'Berlin,' said Mr Tal, 'Berlin is a deserted city.'

'It *is now*,' observed Porlock, finally opening his book.

'Bastard!' cursed Painter, nursing poor Cyclops.

'To *interrupt* the world,' said Mr Tal, '– that was the intention of Joshua: to stab the world in the heart.' This time he poked the air.

'Joshua?' said Porlock, without looking up, 'I fear you shall find, Herr Tal, that you may *not* be Joshua.'

Mr Tal appeared to consider this. He then took out a piece of paper, a kind of certificate, and pointed at a name. 'Benjamin Walter,' it said. He pointed to say *that* was who he found he was.

> When Walter Benjamin died, as an unknown fugitive in the Spanish border town of Port Bou, there was, for some reason, a bureaucratic error that led to the inversion of his name in all official documents relating to his death.

'Benjamin Walter?' said Porlock, head still bowed. 'Why *no*, you are Tal, O.E. Tal. Does it not all come back to you?'

Mr Tal looked at his case. He looked suspicious. Then he turned to me. 'You shall now become,' he whispered, 'the first person to learn my new pseudonym.' He looked away, and back again: '"O.E. Tal," he resumed, 'is an anagram of the Latin "*lateo.*"'

'Meaning?' I whispered.

'"I conceal myself,"' he said.

He breathed, then said again: '"I conceal myself."'

I understood.

**Figure 4.1**
Walter Benjamin in the Bibliothèque Nationale, Paris, 1937.
It is, I am persuaded, a girl who appears in the background.
The copyright is "Photo Gisèle Freund/IMEC/ Fonds MCC."

## SCENE FOUR

# THE FRONT ROOM

'It says here,' muttered Porlock, 'that "Benjamin Walter *died* today."'

The four of us were now scattered across the front room, the room with the television set, before which I sat, on the floor, cross-legged. My back was to the men, but I could see their reflections in the unlit grey-green screen.

'It says here,' muttered Porlock again, 'that "Benjamin Walter *died* today."'

'I beg your pardon?' said a man who stood outside in the front garden but was leaning in at an open window. He said he was a rent collector.

'"Benjamin Walter *died*,"' muttered Porlock yet again, '"Died *today*." It says so here.' He waved a piece of paper. 'We stole it in the night,' he confessed, 'under an indifferent moon, from the sleeping frame of Herr Tal. Do you not remember?' Painter shook his head. He did not remember.

We all turned to stare at the late Benjamin Walter. He was sitting at the high wooden table and was trying, as if hid in a library, to file tiny paper-cuttings within a tiny shoebox. Very soon, his clammy palms were stamped with newspaper print. But he seemed indifferent to the fate of his palms or, indeed, to the fact that one table leg was shorter than the others and constantly shook as he laboured. Under the table stood Mr Tal's case, now so swollen I considered it an H-Bomb.

Mr Tal bent double over one particular cutting. It was an advertisement and announced, in the most reckless of type, or font, that this week was 'National Corset Week.' Mr Tal ran his fingers and eyes over the hand-drawn picture that appeared in the middle of the cutting; it was a sketch of a miraculous woman who wore only a corset and whose hands were ever-so slightly lifted, as if she were about to flee some elegant party that had just grown dull or even terrible. I could see she meant the world to Mr Tal; but not to Porlock, who was still enjoying the excellent joke of 'the Jew's untimely death.'

'Herr Tal,' began Porlock, 'I hate to cause alarm, but it appears you are *dead*. To be precise (and about death one must usually be precise) it seems you died in er . . . ' (he looked down again at the piece of paper) '– Ah yes, in a hotel somewhere in the Pyrenees, at the very edge of the Mediterranean.'

'Nice,' said the rentman at the window. 'I do so love the sea.'

*West Herts and Watford Observer*
August 20, 1954

> On Saturday last it was all smiles for the Oxhey Estate's 'Happy Housewives' (or the 'Double H Club,' as they like to be known) who enjoyed a splendid day out at Southend-on-Sea.

The rentman carried on. He represented, he said, the Council but was also, he said, One of Us, which made him, he said, a species of double agent. He was short and wiry but his arms were long, very long, and he had absurd teeth. Slapstick teeth, he said. Much like his outsize nose and a pair of glasses that did not and would not sit straight. National Health, he said. Over one arm he had a gabardine raincoat and under his other was tucked a huge ledger, as if a Bible. Leather bound, he said – as if leather were a place, or destination. He wore a suit that was, he confessed, on the small side, the small side of things. Indeed, his trousers could not quite reach his shoes, try as ever they might; although three loyal pens stood to attention in the top pocket of his jacket. Here was a thin comedian; a man who appeared about to tell the last joke in Europe.

Porlock, however, believed himself already in possession of such. He was stretched out on the little settee. '*Painter's* settee,' he admitted. And again, Porlock began to read out what was, evidently, a hotel bill. After but a few words, he stopped and looked around. 'It is in Spanish,' he said.

'Perhaps,' said Mr Tal, 'the Holy Ghost will translate it for you.'

'The Holy Who?' inquired the rentman.

'The Holy Ghost,' said Mr Tal.

'No,' said Porlock, from the settee. God, he said, should not be trusted with a hotel bill. Not after all that had happened.

The rentman looked aghast.

'Leave the translation to *me*,' added Porlock. He reclined still further and began:

'*Hotel de Francia.*
Port-Bou, October 1, 1940.

Bill - Dr Benjamin Walter. Items:

1. Room and evening meal for four days.
2. Five lemonades.
3. Four telephone calls.
4. Chemist.
5. Clothing the corpse.
6. Whitewashing walls, disinfecting the room, cleaning the mattress.'

'Filthy sod,' said Painter. He was still buried in his overcoat, but was now entangled with a bike that stood upside down in the middle of the room. He cherished the bike as if it were a wife.

'I wish he'd have his mattress cleaned *now*.' A voice from upstairs. It was that girl again. Her name, they said, was Johanna, Johanna with an 'h,' the 'h' to be heard, and these words of hers were pursued by a man who did nothing but laugh.

'It is, though, a comfort,' said the rentman, 'to think that this-here dead lodger could make a few last calls before falling off –' (he nudged his glasses) '– off, off of the beautiful Pyrenees.'

'But to *who*,' said Painter, 'to *who*,' he span a beloved back wheel, 'to who the hell did he speak?'

'"To *whom*," sweet moron, "To *whom*,"' said Porlock. 'To *whom* did he telephone in his last and desperate hours, minutes and seconds? To *whom*?'

'To whom, indeed,' said the rentman. His eyes narrowed.

And, as they narrowed, Mr Tal looked up from the table that shook. 'Every hour,' he said, 'the telephone was my twin brother.'

'He's got a twin brother?' said the rentman. Alarmed.

'"Twin brother,"' said Porlock, 'is but a metaphor.'

'Or telephone is,' said the rentman.

'Is what?' I asked.

'A metaphor,' said the rentman.

Mr Tal went back to his shoebox. 'These Londoners,' he said, 'have no telephones.'

'So, why call *London*?' muttered Painter. He addressed an innertube.

Pause.

Mr Tal's head was trembling as he bent to open his case. Then he seemed to remember something, or someone, and looked, instead, in the pockets of his jacket.

Mr Tal stumbled first through one and then the other. Finally, he pulled out a Lilliputian notebook along with a collection of cinema tickets over which he had written in the minutest hand. Several of the tickets slipped through his fingers. These too were trembling, and he seemed to be looking for one ticket in particular. When he found the one ticket, he squinted and read it aloud: 'Theodor and Gretel Wiesengrund-Adorno, 21 Palace Court, Hyde Park, London, W2. Tel: Bayswater 3738.' Mr Tal began to dial in mid-air. His forefinger drew a series of incomplete circles, each circle differently incomplete. He now held an invisible receiver to his ear and awaited an answer. There was not one. He put the receiver down. 'These Londoners,' he said, 'have no telephones.'

'Quite,' said Porlock, 'No telephones in London, none whatsoever.' The arms of Painter's settee appeared to embrace him.

'Deaf ears,' said Painter, 'They turn deaf ears.'

'Turn?' said the rentman, 'Turn to *whom*?'

'Oh, just to sweating Jews who dial from mountain tops,' said Porlock. 'This is, you see, 1940,' he said, and pointed at the date on the hotel bill. 'Not a time to telephone London.'

'Theodor and Gretel Wiesengrund-Adorno. Tel: Bayswater 3738,' repeated Mr Tal. Once again, he fingered the air.

Porlock said that, sadly, he did not know the Adornos, unless they were a music-hall act but dimly recalled.

Mr Tal looked down and dragged his case even closer to his knees. His heavy head dropped forward a little and his chin fell neatly into a raised right hand. Then, quite sudden, he spoke.

'We,' he said, '– we who have died . . . '

'Yes . . . ,' said Porlock, eager for news.

'We who have died . . . ,' said Mr Tal.

'Continue,' urged Porlock, but Mr Tal could not. Not yet. So Porlock returned to the very beginning of things. 'Herr Tal,' he said, 'à *propos* being dead, did it come as something of a surprise?'

'When you are taken unawares,' said Mr Tal, 'by the news of a death, there is, in the first mute shock, the indistinct reproach: did you really not know of this?'

'And did you *really* not know?' asked Porlock, 'Did you really not know of your own annihilation?'

'Who *does*?' said the rentman, 'Who *does*?'

'Does what?' asked Porlock.

'Know he has died,' said the rentman.

'Tal bloody does,' said Painter.

'We who have died –,' said Mr Tal.

'*See*!' said Painter. Victory was his, Victor Painter. He had an ear to his innertube.

There was a pause, a pause as Mr Tal studied the arrangements for National Corset Week. The table shook. Mr Tal then turned the cutting over, gently, so gently, and read aloud, very slowly, the newsprint that he found on the far side of the corseted lady. He read:

> *West Herts and Watford Observer*
> April 3, 1953
> At the opening of the Methodist Church Hall on the LCC Oxhey estate the guest speaker, Dr Irvonwy Morgan of the London Methodist Mission, spoke of the challenge that lay ahead. He told the packed hall that "You have the Words of Life, the Words of Life for *those who are dying but do not know it*.'

'Quite,' said Porlock, 'But you, Herr Tal, are *dead* and yet do not seem to know it. What would Dr Morgan have to say about that?'

'The medium,' said Mr Tal, 'obeys the voice that takes possession of him.'

'Wrong!' said Porlock, a clock on the hour. 'Be trying again.'

'There is,' said Mr Tal, 'only one radical novelty – death.'

'Wrong again!' said Porlock. Quite the quiz master. He leaned forward and was about to stub his cigarette out on Mr Tal's cheek when the rentman whispered in his ear that Mr Tal may have a point – 'In the sense,' whispered the rentman, 'that death round here *is*, as so it happens, the rarest of birds.'

> 'We were all so young when we moved in that I never saw a funeral on the estate, and it was some years before I knew anyone who had died.'

'So true,' reflected Porlock. 'It is, come to think of it, not wholly unlike Eden out here.'

'Just like,' said the rentman. He straightened his glasses, one long thin arm extended.

I now abandoned the television set, gravitated to the window, looked outside and watched as a hearse with a tiny coffin on board disappeared up the road at terrible speed. I thought it might be chasing a burglar, or that maybe something had been forgotten. No one else seemed to see it and certainly not Porlock, who said that, by the way, he'd had quite enough of Eden, and that, 'Besides, *someone* must have died – *someone* from round here, *someone* other than the adventurous Herr Tal.' Pause. 'If we can but stay calm,' added Porlock, 'we shall surely think of *someone* who is unequivocally dead.'

'Who?' said Painter, 'Name *one*.'

'And we *shall*,' said Porlock, 'We *can* and we *shall*.'

From under his bicycle (it still stood on its head), Painter dragged out a sheet of well-printed paper. He then read aloud: '"The Use of a Questionnaire on the

Oxhey Housing Estate," *The Medical Officer*, 1957. "APPENDIX II – The Questionnaire."'

'I'm "Regular,"' said the rentman, 'Whatever the question, and whomsoever the questioner, please consider me quite, quite "Regular."'

'"Question Number 1,"' read Painter, '"Have any of the following died? Mother, Father, Brother, Sister. Please put a ring around any that have died."'

We all folded our foreheads desperate to think of any that had died. Foreheads turned to corrugated iron.

'Well,' said the rentman, at last, 'We've certainly had some we had been *thinking* were all dead and quite gone.'

*West Herts and Watford Observer*
September 17, 1954
OXHEY ESTATE TENANT TELLS
WARTIME STORY

Mr. George Thomas, of Seacroft Gardens, Oxhey LCC estate, has quite a story to tell. On September 5, 1943 he was a gunner on a British bomber from No. 103 Squadron that crashed in France. All members of the crew miraculously survived and each then had a series of nerve-wracking adventures. In the case of Mr. Thomas this included travelling south through occupied France to join a party of servicemen and refugees that attempted to make the treacherous journey across the Pyrenees and into neutral Spain. They then spent five days and nights wandering lost in the bitter cold of the Pyrenees winter before they were finally spotted by a German border patrol and arrested. It was not until some weeks later that Mr. Thomas learnt that the party had, without realizing it, walked eight miles into Spanish territory. By the time of his capture

> Mr. Thomas was officially presumed dead, and his wife was just about to draw her first war-widow's pension when news came that he was still alive.

'For instance?' said Porlock.

'Fr'instance,' said Painter, 'that bugger George Thomas. *Nearly* dies, he does.'

'Who does?' asked the rentman.

'This bugger that's not really dead,' said Painter.

'What, *Mr. Tal*?' said the rentman.

'No, you arse,' said Painter, '– that bloke down Seacroft Gardens.'

'But you said he was up the Pyrenees,' said the rentman.

'They *both* were,' said Painter.

'Both were *what*?' said the rentman.

'Up the Pyrenees,' said Painter.

'Doing what, exactly?' said the rentman.

'Bloody dying, or nearly bloody dying,' said Painter.

'As the case may be,' said Porlock.

Pause.

'A bit crowded then?' said the rentman.

'Where?' said Porlock.

'Up the Pyrenees,' said the rentman.

'Certainly,' said Porlock, who hoped for an end to the Pyrenees question.

Pause.

'But I thought he *wasn't* actually dead?' said the rentman.

'Who?' asked Porlock.

'Mr. Tal,' said the rentman.

'No, *he* was dead. Or *is*,' said Porlock. 'It's this Mr *Thomas* who failed to die.'

'So,' said the rentman, 'to clarify: that bloke round Seacroft Gardens is *not* altogether dead?'

'No,' said Porlock, 'not altogether.'

Pause.

And so, there we were, in Eden, looking out, said Porlock, for a local Adam, a first-to-be-dead-and-stay-being-dead. Eager to help, Mr Tal descended into his box of cuttings, but all he pulled out was another advertisement; this time for the perfect pair of trousers, Isaac Walton's Invincible Specials, 49s 6d a pair. Leaving my post at the window, and squinting over Mr Tal's shoulder, I read that not even long sunny days by the sea would cause the Invincible Trousers to lose colour. I stared at a drawing of the Invincible Trousers; no one was in the Trousers and yet they were still walking, all on their own, by the sea, not losing colour. No sign of the dead here, I thought; far from it. But then, quick as ever you like, Mr Tal abandoned the Trousers and fumbled for yet another cutting and waved it in the air. Peace in our time, I thought. Mr Tal then began to read. He read this:

> *West Herts and Watford Observer*
> August 21, 1953
>
> Young Derek Henderson, aged just six, of Hallows Crescent, South Oxhey, died after his shirt caught fire as he sat alone before an open gas-oven door.

'The door,' said Porlock, 'is always open.' Mr Tal nodded and read on. On, on.

> Derek's father, a former fishmonger, now a hospital porter, had gone off to work, and so too Derek's mother, a waitress. 'He had asked me to light the oven because he was cold,' she explained. She had left the house at 7.40 a.m. but expected her husband to be back soon.

Porlock smiled, and Mr Tal continued.

> By 7.50 a.m. a neighbour, a Mrs. Florence Dixon, was woken by screams and a knock at her door. Derek was standing there alight.

Mr Tal lifted his head. 'The child behind a door,' he said, 'is himself the door.' He then straightened his tie and resumed his reading.

> Young Derek later died in hospital, at 6 p.m. The doctor said that 'all the while Derek's burns were being dressed he was conscious, co-operative and very very brave.'

'Derek Henderson,' said Porlock, ' . . . this all-too-conscious boy-at-the-door' (he raised an invisible hat) ' . . . he is our very first to die.'

There was everywhere silence, everywhere.

'But what,' I said, '– what about that girl?' I said how a girl I knew had died of asthma, I had heard, when out with her family on the golf-course, I had heard, and how her father held her in his arms, I had heard, while he waited for the ambulance while it raced all the way from Watford while he prayed while she struggled to breathe and while and while and while all the children of the estate gripped their collars . . . .

> ' . . . The Sunday School lesson that sticks most in my mind was when we were told that one of the girls that usually came had died. I am ashamed, though, to say that I can't remember her name. . . .'

'Susan, Susan Jackman,' I said, 'That was her name, and her father, they say, as he waited for the ambulance, they say, was all the while, trying to work out, they say, if he still believed in our God.' He does, he doesn't. Tick tock. He does, he doesn't. Tick tock.

'Such,' said Porlock, 'are the benefits of having time upon one's hands.'

There was a pause. And then we all, at once, were buried beneath a hailstorm of wild-electric song. A record player spun upstairs, and music fell head-first down the stairs and wound itself around disastrous words – words like, very like, 'leopard-skin pill-box hat.'

When the music at last ceased to career and tumble, Porlock returned to how very similar it All was to Eden around here. 'Yes,' he said, 'quite deathless hereabouts.'

I left Mr Tal at his table, flew to the window, looked outside and saw the very same hearse I had seen just five minutes before. It was still loaded with the tiny coffin and hurtling along, but this time it was going *down* the road.

'Which makes a change,' said Porlock.

'– after London,' said the rentman.

'London,' said Painter, '– death all over.'

Mr Tal nodded. 'There used,' he said, 'to be no house, hardly a room, in which someone had not once died.'

'Or *twice*,' said Porlock.

Pause. Then all, all of us, looked up as strange and struggling sounds fell from Johanna's room. I could still hear the song of the beautiful pillbox hat. 'Honey, can I jump on it some time?' Can I? Can I? Porlock wore a crumbling smile. Mr Tal, though, was adrift and askew. 'Hardly a room,' he said, returning to the dead and all the rooms in which they could be found. 'On this sofa,' he added, 'the aunt cannot but be murdered.'

'You do realize,' said Porlock, 'that your aunt, or indeed, any aunt, dead or undead, is wholly beside the question; as indeed is any relationship they might enjoy with this, or any other, sofa. Though I should prefer to call it a "settee."' Porlock loved this word. He loved it as if an adulterer.

Fair silence followed, or at least it did so here below. Up above, the noise was incurable. Porlock now returned to the riddle of who, exactly, could be murdered on a sofa. He suggested 'The Ruling Class.'

'I beg your soap-box?' said the rentman.

'I think,' said Porlock, 'I think, as ever, of the calamitous Captain Blackwell.'

'And whom's he when he's at whom?' said the rentman.

'Captain Anthony Walter Blackwell,' said Porlock, 'Former owner of the former world that was, formerly, before ever time began, *the* Oxhey Estate, *his* Oxhey Estate – his and no-one else's.'

'Until buggered,' said Painter, he raised a spanner to the light, '– until buggered by his own bloody gun. Breech blew off.'

> In the Spring of 1944 a long public hearing was held at the Watford Town Hall to debate the compulsory purchase order on the Blackwells' Oxhey estate. Many voices were raised in protest, not least that of Captain Blackwell's young widow who argued that to cut down the woods of her estate would remove, as she put it, 'one of London's last remaining lungs.'

'She wouldn't have it,' said Painter. He blew his nose.

'*Who* wouldn't?' asked the rentman.

'Widow Twankey,' said Painter.

'Exchange Cockneys for oak-trees,' said Porlock, 'and London, poor consumptive London, would soon – so reasoned the widow – grow short of breath.'

'Our *coming*,' said Mr Tal, looking through his shoebox, 'Our coming was expected on earth . . . '

'Though not, perhaps, in Watford,' suggested Porlock.

Mr Tal shook his head. '*We*,' he insisted, looking around the room, '*We* have been endowed with Messianic power.'

> *West Herts and Watford Observer*
> December 12, 1954
> At Thursday's Ruridecanal Conference the Rev R.R. Davies, speaking on the topic of 'Some Modern Heresies,' informed local clergy that a large number of heresies prevailed in Watford, in particular Communism, which had taken Christian ideas and put them in a different key. The Communists taught, said Rev. Davies, that the working class would be the Messiah or Saviour of history.

Painter stared at his bike and murmured, saying, as if suddenly possessed, that 'every worker is a new bloody Jesus.' Porlock, smoothing his hair, said that he was not so certain of this; nor was he entirely convinced that 'this particular Jesus, Mr. Jesus Painter, did *any* work these days.' The rentman, however, remarked that he, for one, altogether welcomed the prospect of 'so many Saviours.' He did then confess that he was 'Not quite sure what they would *do* all day. But perhaps,' he added, 'some clue or hint would be forthcoming at the very next meeting of –' (he coughed) '– the Party.'

> 'My father was a life-long Communist and often he organized political discussions on the estate, usually in our front room. I was only a child but sometimes I was allowed to sit in on the meetings . . . '

'Ah, the Party,' said Porlock, 'The Party to end all parties.' He brushed clean the shoulders of his world. Painter said nothing. And still he said nothing as he moved towards the rentman at the window. And so I stepped aside not wanting, as yet, to be killed alive, and watched as Painter stooped to the level of the rentman and asked if he, the rentman, could see his way to overlooking the present week's bleeding rent.

The rentman winked, tapped his nose, winked again and pointed up the wicked stairs. Painter coughed violently and battered at his cursed chest.

Pause.

The rentman now turned to Porlock and suggested that he relate, on behalf of the People and for the benefit of All, and Mr Tal in particular, the full and utter history of Anthony Blackwell, esquire.

Porlock raised a thumb. 'You see, Herr Tal,' he said, 'Captain Blackwell is to be compared, I say, to your aunt, the one so-murdered on the sofa. Or, let us say, "the settee."' Mr Tal looked as if he was about to confess to something but Porlock carried on: '– the point of comparison being that Blackwell also haunts settees, in particular the settees of this our ashen-faced estate.' He smiled again.

I stared hard at the settee, but could see no trace of either Aunt or Captain, whether murdered or not. It then came to me that I probably would not recognize a dead person if I saw one, since I didn't really know any dead people, unless one counted Jesus, who I did feel I knew but, then, He was alive again.

I explained all this to Mr Tal who paused and then replied, observing that, 'Even in times of narrowly prejudiced thought there was an inkling that life was not limited to organic corporeality.'

Bewildered, I nodded; but Painter, once more entangled with his trembling bike, appeared to understand, announcing that he would be having no religious maniacs under *his* bloody roof.

The rentman observed that the bloody roof was not, technically, Painter's roof, but that it belonged to the

Council, as was evidenced, he would like to add, by the guttering that was dripping right now, even as he spoke, onto his (the rentman's) head. This was, he noted, the exact same guttering that had been broken for some weeks now, notwithstanding innumerable invitations to his colleagues from the said Council to pop along and kindly mend it.

Painter declared he would try again, vowing he would shelter no religious maniacs under a roof that was *not* bloody his and *never* would be.

'Beautiful,' said the rentman. He used a handkerchief to wipe the rain from his spectacles. He could have done, he said, with windscreen wipers.

Pause.

'We who have died,' said Mr Tal, 'are resurrected in what happens to us.'

'Really?' said the rentman.

Mr Tal nodded. 'We are resurrected,' he repeated, 'in what happens to us.'

'But,' said the rentman, '*nothing* happens to us.'

'Exactly,' said Porlock, 'Ours is a quiet resurrection. Quiet so quiet.'

'No,' said Painter, 'Not quiet, not here, not Little Moscow.'

'I think,' said Porlock, 'that Painter should see no more of his Comrades.'

'But what,' whispered the rentman, 'would poor Mr. P. do after dark? Alone as he is now.'

Painter touched the broken heart of his bicycle. He seemed not to hear.

'Has he not considered,' said Porlock, 'the Evening Institute?' There, he had heard, they did 'interesting things with lampshades.'

'The choice is clear,' agreed the rentman, struggling to keep dry his skull, 'It is World Revolution OR –' (here he paused) '– *Interested Lampshades*.' Thin comedian, he was.

'Alternatively,' announced Porlock, 'All sides could come to a devastating compromise and agree to incinerate a well-made effigy of Winston Churchill.'

*West Herts and Watford Observer*
November 7, 1954

It was bonfire night with a difference for the women's section of the Oxhey Labour Party as they burnt an effigy not of Guy Fawkes but of Sir Winston Churchill. When asked about this Mrs. A. Pond replied, 'It took two and a half hours to make but then there's nothing else to do – that's the trouble with the estate.'

## SCENE FIVE

# STILL THE FRONT ROOM

It was later. The bicycle had gone. Painter sat on a stiff-backed chair that had wandered to the middle of the room. He held an unopened newspaper. Porlock, now smoking, still enjoyed the settee's embrace. Mr Tal was bent, as before, over the cuttings, spread far across the high wooden table. The rentman still leaned at the window from without. I sat on a chair that I had taken to the window, and looked out over and beyond the rentman's shoulder.

'You know,' said Porlock, inhaling, 'I think we may have somewhat lost our bearings.'

'Lost,' said Painter, 'Lost in the woods . . . . Bloody trees.'

'He believes,' whispered the rentman, 'that the woods grow ever closer.'

'Do they not?' said Porlock.

Pause.

'You know,' said Porlock, 'I think we may have somewhat lost our bearings.'

Pause.

'Once,' Porlock continued, 'we used to consider the question of what it is To Be No More. You recall?'

The rentman said he recalled.

'Well, *now*,' declared Porlock, '– right now, it is time we *resumed* our investigation, our investigation of the art of dying.'

'About which,' said the rentman, 'we certainly have our inklings.'

'You allude, I shall insist,' said Porlock, 'to those among us who staged but a few hours ago a tearful production of Frank Harvey's *The Poltergeist . . . .*'

RENTMAN: Ah, tender nights!

PORLOCK: And such tender possession, in that ghost-shaken Vicarage.

*(Pause)*

PAINTER: *(Opening his newspaper and reading)* 'Among the failings of this production one could list: bad timing, insufficient pace, and too few rehearsals' – *West Herts and Watford Observer, April 16,* 1953.

RENTMAN: Ah, but how many times could anyone rehearse the removal of alien spirits? Or, indeed, and let us be frank –

PORLOCK: Frank Harvey.

RENTMAN: – the moving-on of . . .

PAINTER: The unwanted.

MYSELF: The superfluous.

PAINTER: The beaten.

RENTMAN: The leftie.

PAINTER: The shit.

RENTMAN: The Yid.

*(No noise. Nor movement. For this is a motionless production, each actor remaining in his place – on his chair or settee, at his window or table.)*

RENTMAN: Moreover, how many times can you rehearse, or repeat, the lament:

PAINTER: 'If only we could get back to London!'

PORLOCK: With which the play opens.

RENTMAN: Though does not, alas, immediately close.

PORLOCK: There being yet-to-come two more Acts of haunted crockery inclined to throw itself from a theatrical sideboard.

RENTMAN: Shades of a suicidal Christ. *(A loud crash upstairs.)*

PORLOCK: Not to mention a Poltergeist that itself forever waltzes through the house.

RENTMAN: Shades of Pentecostal breath. *(Another crash.)*

PORLOCK: God, no! It farts around, I say, like . . . *(he quotes the play)*: 'Like the last train from the Elephant and Castle . . . .'

RENTMAN: Not that it *began* as the last train.

PAINTER: No – it just *grew* late, very very late.

*(Silence again.)*

MR TAL: The extremes encompassed within redemption are 'too early' *and* 'too late.'

*(Porlock, Painter and the rentman all freeze at their posts.)*

PORLOCK: Exactly, but let us return now to F. Harvey's jewel of English repertory, and our infinitely under-rehearsed production. Enter stage-left (or possibly stage-right) one Vincent Ebury, member of the Association for Psychical Research of Great Britain.

RENTMAN: Not a clown from the Council?

PAINTER: A damp clown?

PORLOCK: Absolutely not. Or at least, I think not. *(Porlock, for a moment, embraces doubt.)* Whatever, this Visitor, this Wolf at the Door, this Wandering Inspector of Spirits –

RENTMAN (This *Vincent Ebury*, let it be remembered).

PORLOCK: – he sets about purging the haunted house.

PAINTER: *(Wearily)* Purging, purging, purging.

PORLOCK: An Herculean act of clearance. An act otherwise known –

RENTMAN: In the forlorn words of the forlorn Vicar –

PORLOCK: As . . .

PAINTER: 'Hunting the bogies.'

PORLOCK: Or, again:

PAINTER: 'Catching sunbeams with a shovel.'

PORLOCK: Or even . . .

RENTMAN: In the words of, let us say, a passing cyclist.

PORLOCK: As . . .

PAINTER: The moving-on of the tubercular working-class.

PORLOCK Or . . .

RENTMAN: The dispersal, and thus emasculation, of an hitherto radical urban proletariat. (*All pause to admire the rentman.*)

PORLOCK: In short, in sum, and in quite other words, the . . .

MR TAL: School of exile.

PORLOCK: Please, please; no political allegory – there is, out here, already sufficient mirth. No, we must insist that this our disastrous play is but an everyday story of everyday catastrophe *(more crashing is heard above)* . . . of just another haunted house . . . *(yet more crashing, and by now Porlock is having to shout)* . . . of just another world longing to return to the dear and dead centre that, alas, cannot hold.

PORLOCK, PAINTER, RENTMAN: Oh, oh, to return to London!

The three men fell silent, and I thought their theatre had finished. But then, without preamble, Porlock rose to his feet and took on the character of the Vicar's befuddled neighbour: 'I am,' (he quoted) 'but an ordinary sort of bloke!' He then spread wide his arms and cried, ' . . . Just a man who believes in living in one world at a time!'

I applauded. How right he was.

'Ah yes, but you know what it is, Sir,' chirped the rentman (he was now Olive, the Vicar's trusty maid) '– When you're old, heaven seems just across the street.'

'Bollocks,' said Painter, 'It's just across *the railway line*.'

'On the estate, back in the early days, we used to call our bit of the railway line the Jordan River . . . '

'Beyond which,' said Porlock, 'lies the *private* estate, that Elysian redoubt they call "Heaven in Hertfordshire."' He returned to the warm settee and lay himself out.

'But,' said the rentman, growing deep, 'is Heaven not so much *across* the street as *on* the street?'

Mr Tal nodded at this, although without looking up from the table. 'Someone,' he said, 'kneels on the asphalt in the busiest of streets and draws the figure of Christ.'

'You know,' said the rentman, tapping at his teeth, 'he does sound like a book.'

'Which is,' said Porlock, 'precisely what the Insurance Man remarks in this our regrettable drama.'

'Ironical,' whispered the rentman, 'Ironical.'

Silence.

It was now raining hard, and for once there was peace. Peace enough to hear a million birds begin to sing. Painter, still on his chair, put his hands to his ears and said they sounded like a crown of bloody thorns. Five minutes passed and then he dragged his hands from his ears and returned to the subject of streets.

'Streets?' he said, 'We have no streets – only roads, empty pointless roads. Out here, no crowds, no traffic, no fights, no whores.'

Porlock coughed an angel's cough, as if wishing perhaps to demur.

'We do, though,' said the rentman, 'have Weather. Or, rather, rain.' He looked to the apologetic sky. 'And not,' he added, 'just any rain.' He put on his gabardine raincoat. 'This here is *experimental* rain.' The Council, he said, had chosen the estate to carry out a very special Rain-Fall Run-Off Experiment.

'Bugger rain!' said Painter, 'What of that Poltergeist? What of him?' Painter got to his stiffening feet and began to walk the room.

'Ah,' said Porlock, 'I cannot recall. It being so long ago. Like everything.'

'But you must know?' said Painter, '– must know what happened.'

'Or at least,' said the rentman, 'what it all *meant*?' He crossed his eyes.

'Meant?' said Porlock.

'Yes, *meant*,' said the rentman. He uncrossed his eyes.

'I should imagine –,' began Porlock.

'Yes yes,' urged the rentman.

'I should imagine,' Porlock went on, 'it was something to do with –'

'No bullshit now,' begged Painter. Halting for an instant.

'Just tell it as it was,' said the rentman, '– as in the play, very word for very word.'

Porlock nodded. It was, he said, something to do with how the laws of physics are suspended in the presence of certain people.

'People?' said the rentman.

'In short,' said Porlock, 'something to do with the power of *thought*.'

'Thought?' I said.

'Yes – you know: think, think,' cried the rentman. He hopped a little, at the window.

Pause.

'The main thing,' whispered Mr Tal, 'is to learn *crude* thinking – that is, the thinking of the great.' He filed another cutting.

'Who, though,' said the rentman, 'thinks out here, out here in Heaven?'

'But,' said Painter, '*that's* why we're here.' He halted again and drew out from under the settee a ragged screw of papers, the very image of a doll, a rag doll. He began to read: '"Some Problems in the Collection and Analysis . . . "'

'Paralysis?' said the rentman.

'– *Analysis*,' said Painter, 'Analysis of Morbidity Data.'

'Christ!' said Porlock.

'– Obtained From a Sample Survey,' concluded Painter. He was now ready to read from the Analysis itself. He opened his lungs and began: '"It seems relevant here,"' he read.

'What, *here*?' asked the rentman. He was lost in Heaven.

'Yes, *here*,' said Painter. He felt he must begin again. '"It seems relevant here . . . "'

'Christ!' said Porlock, 'Christ go quickly!'

'"To discuss,"' continued Painter, '"what other methods we could have used to stimulate people"' (he paused) '" . . . to *think*."'

Painter looked up from the doll, the rag doll. He had won. 'See,' he said, 'we've been dumped out here to bloody think, to do nothing but bloody think. Stands to reason. There's bugger-else to do.'

Porlock stood up and took hold of Painter's doll. Porlock glanced down at the paper infant, looked up again and said that the unbending author of 'Some Problems in the Collection and Analysis etc. etc.' had simply desired (he read aloud from hereon) 'to stimulate people to think . . . ' (he paused as if on a stage) ' . . . *about their ill-health*.'

Painter reached for his chair.

'We have,' said Porlock, 'been brought here to think *ill*, to think the illness of ourselves.' He lay once more on the settee. 'You see, for the likes of us, there is no philosophy; indeed, no literature – only such unforgettable works as . . . ' (he struggled to remember) ' . . . such unforgettable works as . . . ' (it came to him at last) 'as "Incidents of Neurosis in a New Housing Estate."'

Painter, defeated, sat once more on his chair.

'But what,' said the rentman, 'what of Mr. F. Harvey's theatrical jewel?'

'Pure farce,' said Porlock, 'pure spiritual farce. And when, in the end, its adulterous trousers finally fall about its shuddering ankles all we are left with is –'

'What?' said Painter. 'What?'

'The *girl*,' said Porlock, 'the girl in the house. *She* is left. It will, you see, have all revolved about *her*. She, they all say, is "The Agent of Energy."'

Pause.

'Had she touched me,' said Mr Tal, 'with the match of her eyes, I should have gone up like a magazine.'

Pause.

I gave up my post at the window, gave it up for dead, for it was time, time, I knew, time at last, to switch on the television set. As I waited for the picture to come, Johanna appeared, sweeping gravity from her eyes. She said that her boyfriend, Romeo, was around the back and that he was smoking a final cigarette. For a moment, I thought she was about to sit beside me on the floor by the television, but she headed for Mr Tal. He still sat at the table and she bent over him and kissed his head. Clumsy head.

'Romeo's last sigh,' said Mr Tal, not looking up, '– Romeo's last sigh flitted through our back yard.'

*Carpenders Park Station*

**Figure 6.1**
Railway platform, Oxhey Estate, c. 1952.
Romeo, as if the young man in the foreground.

## SCENE SIX

# THE GARDEN IN THE EVENING

The garden stormed my mind, it being all overgrown, a mirror of chaos. There were, however, a few visitant forms and orderly shapes – the washing-line, a fence, a swing. And then there were things that should not have been there at all: a fragment of carpet, a stray settee and a standard lamp. Some person, I thought, had taken time to arrange these things so that they should have the appearance of a lounge, a ghost of a lounge. And this stiff spectre glared forever towards the back of the house, which stormed my mind still more for around the kitchen door was a sea of crazy paving, although crazy only in name since, again, some person had clearly laboured long to impose both order and design. At last, towards the corner of the garden, was a tree, and within its folds stood Johanna. She wore dark glasses. Hidden, behind this night, was the match of her eyes.

*Modern Housing Estates:*
*A Practical Guide to their Planning,*
*Design and Development*

> The presence of a tree in a garden is likely to encourage the tenant's interest both in his own garden and in other trees on the estate.

Mr Tal looked at the tree and, beyond it, at all the trees in the woods. It was a late summer's evening. Beautiful, beautiful enough to die.

'The landscape,' whispered Mr Tal, 'sends us our beloved.' He nodded at me. 'It knows but one girl, and she is already a woman.' Johanna stared back and lit a cigarette. The smoke from between her lips rose twisted and curled. 'She is,' said Mr Tal, 'the "Madonna with the Cigarettes."'

Mr Tal now drew a hammer from his pocket and began the task of nailing to the tree a vast collection of bus tickets. The back of each ticket was covered with miniscule writing. 'Over 600 quotations systematically and clearly arranged,' he said. Again and again, Mr Tal dropped either nail or hammer or ticket, sometimes all three, and every time it happened he would mutter, 'Greetings from Mr. Clumsy, the hunchback.' Mr Clumsy, it seemed, was a terrible friend of Mr Tal's. He was a 'little man,' said Mr Tal, but a little man who loved to see Mr Tal suffer disaster. And disaster he did indeed suffer, for after half an hour Mr Tal had managed to nail just five quotations to the tree.

Mr Tal sighed a terrible sigh, he had been here before. He lay down. The grass was long and there he lay, his legs stretched out, his feet crossed and his head propped up by his briefcase. And I watched as a spider walked across Mr Tal's face and crawled into the corner of his mouth. Then, as the spider re-emerged, Mr Tal spoke once more. Addressing no one in particular, and still horizontal, he said, 'Last night Brecht found me in the garden reading *Das Kapital*.'

I did not know of anyone called Brecht, but I thought that Porlock must do so. He, though, said nothing, being all too busy with dragging a kitchen chair into the garden. He then stood on the chair, winked at me, his little man, and announced that, on behalf of the Evening Institute, he was about to deliver a lecture provisionally entitled, 'The Soul of Boredom.'

I sat on the swing, stilling myself in readiness for 'The Soul.' Painter, however, walked straight past the fellow on the chair. Painter was pushing a bicycle with one hand and with the other he was carrying a spade. Porlock seemed not to notice.

'In this utopian Europe,' said Mr Tal, 'intellectuals weave the text of a sermon undaunted by rows of empty seats.'

Porlock began now to look through all his pockets. He was looking, he said, for the woven text of his particular sermon, and was growing a little frantic as pocket after pocket failed him. He was most desperate, he said, not to disappoint this particular corner of utopian Europe. Empty seats, notwithstanding.

Painter had made his way to the edge of the garden and stood by Johanna's crazy tree. A tiny shower of ash fell, like vengeance, from the tree. Painter leaned his spade against the tree and laid down his bike. This, his darling machine, had 'gone home.' He raised his left hand, made the sign of the cross, reached for his spade, also with his left, and began to dig.

> '. . . I recall a family of six children, neighbours of ours, who together once dug an enormous hole in the back garden to dispense of unwanted bikes. . . .'

Mr Tal looked across at Painter and shrugged. 'He who seeks,' he said, 'to approach his own buried past must conduct himself like a man digging.'

'Ah, but you see,' said the rentman, popping his head out of the kitchen window, 'he's not *like* a man digging, rather he *is* a man digging. A man who actually digs is no more *like* a man who digs than is a man who stands around talking absolute codswallop when he should in fact be collecting rent.'

Nothing. The rentman changed buses and tried announcing the End of the World in a cheery voice. Nothing again, so he said he would be putting the kettle on. Straightaway, Porlock stopped journeying through his pockets – 'Ah, the indispensable brew,' he said.

'No less indispensable,' said Mr Tal, 'is the cautious probing of the spade in the dark loam.'

*West Herts and Watford Observer*
June 25, 1950

> On Saturday Lady Paterson, President of the Oxhey Estate Horticultural Society, presented the prizes to both Members and Members' Wives at the Society's first ever 'Produce Show.' The Society was disappointed that just 160 individuals had exhibited but then many of the tenants had never had a garden before and the local soil is described as 'starved.'

'This earth,' said Painter, 'is sodden, sodden clay.' He coughed as if he were no longer human. 'This too, too solid bloody earth,' he added.

Mr Tal nodded and said something about 'The reliability of English ground.'

'But *how* reliable,' asked Porlock, turning on the clumsy man, '– how reliable is English ground if one is not oneself of English *blood*?'

'Or just plain bonkers?' cried the rentman, from the kitchen.

'Or *dead*?' I said.

Mr Tal felt for his case. 'The trembling treetops,' he said, 'assail us with questions.'

'So they do,' said the Madonna busy smoking in the tree. 'And here is another: Who, who is that wizened dwarf?'

'Theology,' said Mr Tal.

'No,' she said, 'The little man, who's he? The hunchback?'

'Theology,' said Mr Tal.

I began to explain that my name was John.

'Like *Saint* John,' said Porlock.

'What, Saint John off the Cross?' shouted the rentman, from the kitchen.

'You mean St John *of* the Cross,' shouted Porlock.

'Do I?' shouted the rentman.

'Anyway,' I said, 'it's "*Johnny*" really, my family call me "Johnny."'

'Johnny Homeless,' muttered Mr Tal.

'Though my real name is Stephen,' I added. 'I was christened Stephen John.'

'He looks like Derek Henderson to me,' said Painter.

'No,' I protested, but Mr Tal shook his head. 'The child,' he said, 'becomes a ghost.'

'Exactly,' said Porlock, turning to me, '*You*,' he said, 'are barely here.' Porlock explained that I was 'barely here' in the sense that I was not born of London, and that my father was only here because, said Porlock, 'he seeks to recover our misplaced souls. Your father desires, let us not beat about the burning bush, that we be recalled to life, rescued as from an everlasting bonfire or, at the very least, from eternal and absolute boredom. Am I not right?'

'I think so,' I said, as I began to swing on the swing, 'I think so, yes.'

*West Herts and Watford Observer*
June 19, 1953

It is all go on the Oxhey estate, where St Martin's Presbyterian Church is fast being built in Muirfield Road; above the east end of the Church will be a floodlit wooden cross visible to all.

'Bloody churches,' said Painter, 'Time was we were –'

'Free,' said Mr Tal, 'free of the chimes that on Sunday spread such deep melancholy.'

> 'I remember, before the church was built, that we used to have an open-air Sunday School, lit illegally with an extension cable from a house. The Women's Meeting was led by a lady who used to sit on a beer-barrel.'

'Holy Shit!' cried someone, 'Holy Shit! Shit! Shit!' It was someone stood at an upper window. The curtains were closed, although the window was open, and whoever cried shit-upon-the-world had made the curtains swirl and swell.

'Proust,' observed Mr Tal.

'Beg your dish-cloth?' cried the rentman, from the kitchen.

'Proust,' said Mr Tal, 'devoting all his hours to work in his darkened room.'

'No, I don't think it's Proust,' cried the rentman. 'I think you'll find it's Romeo.'

'Bloody Spiv,' said Painter, 'bloody Spiv.'

> *West Herts and Watford Observer*
> May 11, 1951
> On Sunday last the Oxhey Estate Fellowship held its very first Empire Youth Day Service. The address was given by Mr. F.C. Sage who commented that 'The greatest menace to this great nation of ours are Fifth Columnists and Spivs.'

Suddenly, and without warning, two or three books flew from the darkened room and fell to the garden below, clean through the evening light. The books missed

Porlock by hardly an inch. He was smoking and still stood on the kitchen chair, oblivious, cigarette in hand.

'Blooming Romeo,' cried the rentman, addressing Mr Tal, 'I do believe he's unpacking your library.' Two more books descended. 'Hard rain,' cried Romeo. There was, though, little surprise at this falling of the sky: Painter continued with his grave, Johanna turned her head away, and I swung angelic into the guilt-red sky.

Just then, the rentman popped out from the kitchen. Could anyone see their way to lending him a shilling? For the meter, the gas meter.

'The Vienna gas board,' said Mr Tal, 'has stopped supplying gas to the Jews'

'Clowns,' said Painter.

'The Jews,' said Mr Tal, 'used the gas mainly –' (he paused) '– for the purpose of committing suicide.'

'Clowns,' said Painter.

'Clowns,' echoed the rentman, and he popped back into the house with a shilling. It had been hurled at him by Porlock, along with a curse. Two minutes later, he came out again, this time with a huge bandage on his thumb. He raised it to signal that all was now well with the meter. As he did so, a book cracked Porlock on the head, and he said that time it was at last to commence his Evening Institute Lecture. The rentman and Mr Tal sat down together, side by side on the settee. The rentman looked as if he could hardly wait for the Lecture to begin, and Mr Tal peered deep into his case. 'The inner workings,' said the rentman, knowingly.

Porlock now kissed his cigarette goodbye, dropped it and stubbed it out with the sole of his shining shoe. Still no laces. Then he was off. 'My subject this evening,' he said, 'is the literary history of Watford. Brief it will inevitably be,' he said, 'but Epic.' He coughed. 'It is true,' he said, 'that Watford is the very soul of the everyday, the commonplace, the dull, the banal, the anodyne.' (He grew hot.) 'A place that might seem forever to urinate upon the privileged moment, the heightened sentiment, the literary anecdote.' (He threw his arms wide and nearly fell off the chair.) 'And yet, and yet, I shall now whisper that our very own and very dear Watford does, yes does,' (he breathed) 'eke out some kind of second life within the far country of –' (he paused then went for a big finale) '– the far, far country of *Literature*!' (He breathed again.) 'And this life, this sweet, sweet second life is, I shall insist –'

'The literary precipitate of a certain form of existence,' suggested Mr Tal.

'Good Heavens,' said Porlock, 'How did *you* know?'

Mr Tal tapped his case as if for good luck. He seemed to like it on the settee.

'Whatever and whatever,' resumed Porlock, 'This second life, this literary life, this life in ink, this life in death, it begins with that great middle-brow wit and self-confessed Idler, Jerome K. Jerome J. K. Jerome K. Jerome.' Porlock was having trouble. 'Author,' he went on, 'of the much-loved *Three Men in A Panic*.' The rentman nodded like a scholar. 'It is, however, an altogether different work of Jerome Jerome's that concerns us this evening, one in which we read that the great Idler was himself (and here I quote) "Pacing the Euston platform late one night waiting for the last train to . . . *Watford*."' Porlock beamed. His teeth were grey. 'Kindly note,' he said, 'that our Watford-bound Idler goes on to spot, alone upon the platform, a man who (and, as ever, I quote) "Was cursing an automatic machine."'

'Never works,' said the rentman, from the settee.

'*Now*,' said Porlock, 'let us not be carried away.'

The rentman said that he wouldn't be.

'Nor let us be overly gleeful,' added Porlock, grey teeth again.

The rentman said he would guard against it.

'For you see,' said Porlock, 'there is, I fear,' (he grew deep, very deep) 'there is, I fear, Something Terrible buried within this late-night Jeromian Moment-in-Watford-Time, a moment in which, to précis: *man – meets – train – meets – man – meets – cursing – meets – machine – meets – very Last and Very Final Train.*'

'I suspected as much,' said the rentman, nudging Mr Tal, his neighbour.

'And this Something Terrible,' continued Porlock, 'is enfolded, much like, say, a curio, inside the little-known fact that the great poet W.H. Audenary' (more trouble) 'had a distant relation, a bank-clerk called Arthur Henry Bicknell who, on February 26, 1881, was sailing through Dalton Junction on the Kensington flyer when said locomotive ran smack-straight into the splendid iron arse of (and once more I quote) ". . . the *Watford* train."'

'Of those who were in the train,' muttered Mr Tal, 'none was rescued.' There was great sadness on the settee.

'I am afraid Herr Tal,' said Porlock, 'you have caught quite the wrong train – for on that day, Hallelujah, *many* were rescued and *many* saved, including dear Arthur Henry Bicknell. However and however, just twelve hours later, after a whole day at work, in the office, as a clerk, humdrum-humdrum, our hero went home, and there died quietly, as only an office-clerk can, from sweet Concussion of the Brain.'

'For the worker,' said Johanna, 'the leisure of death must always await the completion of labour.'

Porlock scratched at his rear – clearly Mr Tal had been instructing the girl. He, though, Dr Porlock, whatever the storm, must carry on.

'Once again,' he said, 'the Watford train proves to be (at least as far as A.H. Bicknell is concerned) quite literally the very last train – or, if you will, the *terminal* train.' Another book struck Porlock on the head, and the rentman observed that Dr Porlock's Lecture was proving 'A fine comic turn.'

'Watford,' replied Porlock, 'is no laughing matter.' Yet another book assaulted him, this time on the nose. 'Though I might,' he continued, 'allow myself a rather alarming smirk at my next deftly-selected literary citation, one which I take from that existential cul-de-sac of a play, *The Carefaker* – by, of course, dear Harold Punter.'

'I know him,' said the rentman, as if addressing the settee.

'Sorry, "Harold *Splinte*r,"' said Porlock.

'And him,' said the rentman, now nudging the settee.

'I mean "*Pinter*," "Harold *Pinter*,"' said Porlock.

'Him and all,' said the rentman, he nudged again.

'Splendid,' said Porlock, 'And who else but the great HP –'

'Sauce!' said the rentman.

'– could have given us a drama,' said Porlock, 'which revolves around the immortal line (as uttered by the immortal tramp): "I took a short cut to Watford and . . . " (Porlock paused) ". . . picked up a pair of shoes."'

'Magical!' enthused the rentman.

'Somewhere,' muttered Mr Tal, 'shoes rain from horns of plenty.'

'Indeed, Herr Tal,' said Porlock, 'And that plenteous somewhere is, I propose, our own and very Watford – a Holding Camp, as it is, for Long-Lost Shoes. However and however, let us not forget the immortal tramp's very next immortal line –'

'No, let us not forget,' said the rentman.

'– Namely . . . ' (Porlock cleared his throat) '"Got onto the North Circular, just past Hendon, and the sole come off, right where I was walking."'

Porlock looked to the settee for an ovation. But, nothing was doing, and off he went again. 'So,' he said, 'what we can now see developing is a Motif, yes, a Motif no less, a Motif that I shall term (if you would indulge me) the, er . . . "train – train – crash – shoe – North Circular – sole – come right off – off the line – off the rails – off his head – off his bloody-rocker"' *Motif.*' Porlock clutched at this final word, final straw. He was drowning.

'Good heavens,' said the rentman. He yawned.

'And this, this, I propose' (Porlock was all hot again) 'is the Great Watford Line, the Great Watford Line of – ' (he paused) '– of Total and Absolute Bloody Disaster!'

'Bravo!' said the rentman.

'I thank you,' said Porlock, 'but I have not yet quite terminated, for this, the Watford line, or even (if you will) the Watford Junction or *con*junction –'

'Beg your soap-suds?' said the rentman, nudging the settee once more.

'– connects effortlessly,' said Porlock, 'with my final and greatest citation. This concerns C.S. Lewis. Well-known Author, of course –'

'Of course,' said the rentman. That was sufficient for him and, indeed, the settee.

'– of *The Iron, the Ditch and the Doorknob*,' said Porlock. He then added, 'Well, as you all know, dear C.S. Suez –'

'A crisis waiting to happen,' said the rentman.

'– once attended,' continued Porlock, 'a small private school in Watford, an establishment he detested with such fine and tender passion that when, late in life and long, long after the great song and dance of World War Two –'

'World War *What*?' said the rentman. He was distracted by the sunset.

'It matters not,' said Porlock, 'the point is that when he, C.S. Suez, looked back upon his schooldays he chose, in all candour, to call Watford "the little town of –" (please wait for the crash) . . . "– the little town of *Belsen*."

'Belsen?' said the rentman. The settee was disturbed.

'Yes "Belsen,"' said Porlock, '"Belsen in Hertfordshire," to be precise.' He shook, toppled from his kitchen chair and tumbled to the earth, searching all pockets for but one cigarette. Painter, meanwhile, hurled his now tangled bike into the enormous great hole he had dug. He then mimed the act of throwing hundreds of other tangled bikes into the pit.

*West Herts and Watford Observer*
May 23, 1945

> On the morning that the newspapers revealed the Nazi atrocities committed at Belsen many Watford people spontaneously demonstrated outside a local hospital for German Prisoners of War.

'Why?' said Mr Tal.

'No. *What?*' said the rentman, 'you mean "What?" . . . "What – what – what"' (the needle stuck) '"– *what* was Belsen?"'

Mr Tal straightened his tie. 'Look,' said the rentman (the thin comedian was dying), 'If you really did kick the bucket before blooming Belsen was – was, well, blooming Belsen – then you will, well, have no idea' (he tapped at his ledger) '– not a clue, not the faintest . . . '

'About what?' I asked

'The Yids,' said the rentman.

Mr Tal straightened his tie.

'You don't have a clue, do you?' said the rentman.

Mr Tal, the settee his vantage point, looked around the garden for a clue. He seemed at last to find one. 'I spoke,' he said, 'with my brother on the telephone.' He paused, before adding, 'Rumours of his death had already surfaced.'

'Well,' said the rentman, 'there are now rumours of –.' He stopped, then started again. 'Well, they are saying,

saying that there are thousands – No, millions, I hear, I hear . . . blooming millions.'

'I can count on my fingers,' offered Mr Tal, getting up.

'No, use mine, please, use mine,' said the rentman. He too stood up, saying he would broadcast the exact number by making a wireless of his fingers. 'Each finger,' he said, 'will stand for . . .' (he breathed) 'a million.' He raised one finger. He then raised a second, and with this one he nudged his lop-sided glasses. National Health, he muttered, before raising a third and then a fourth. Why me? A comedian like me. Why should I have to tell the Jew? The only one that doesn't know. He peered through the bars of his fingers to see how Mr Tal was taking the news. Nothing. The rentman then raised a fifth and arthritic finger. He stared at his own hand as a leper might. Mr Tal took off his glasses and tried hard to clean them with his handkerchief. He returned them to his nose. All the while, the rentman's signifying hand stayed right up close to Mr Tal's face. The old man neither flinched nor even blinked. In fact, he was about to turn and go, as if thinking that the rentman had now finished his fingerly business, when the rentman lifted high his right hand. It was clenched, but then he slowly raised his thumb, the one with the bandage. 'Six,' he said, 'six, six, six million of you.'

'For Christ's sake!' begged Painter.

Pause, there was a pause, I swear there was a pause, and then the rentman announced that he, the rentman, should be running along as the tea would stand in need of pouring. For a moment, I thought Mr Tal was about to tear each of his 600 quotations into 10,000 pieces, but then I saw that he did not despair. Because he did not comprehend.

'Think, Arse, think,' urged Painter, '– like six-million Derek Hendersons, it is. Understand?'

'An old man many times singed,' suggested Mr Tal.

'No! *Burnt*!' said Painter, 'Bloody burnt, burnt, burnt – so bloody burnt that six million ambulances could not have saved them.' I reached for my collar. It was warm with the sliding sun.

Mr Tal looked all around. 'Historical man,' he said, 'has a readiness at all times to recognize that everything can go wrong.'

'You can say that again,' said the rentman, who had just dropped a tray full of tea on to what he called the terrace. Paving, crazy paving. The crash was abroad and everywhere, but only Mr Tal moved to help. I remained at a distance.

'Hopelessly sad,' said Mr Tal, who had bent down and was holding a fragment of china. 'I pick it up,' he said, 'and question it, like Hamlet addressing the skull.' Mr Tal looked across at Painter who was now knee-deep in the pit and quizzing his bike.

*West Herts and Watford Observer*
April 16, 1954

Edward Tully, currently without work but formerly employed as a grave digger, appeared at Watford Magistrates Court accused of stealing from his mother's gas meter. Tully said 'I took the money because I'm fed up with Oxhey.'

Mr Tal was still bent over his fragment. 'I pick it up,' he said, 'and question it, like Hamlet addressing the skull.'

'And *what*,' said the rentman, also bent, '– *what* are you asking your skull?'

'Why?' was Mr Tal's reply.

'Why *what*?' asked the rentman.

'Why the world?' said Mr Tal. He rose and hitched up his trousers.

'Well,' said the rentman, returning to the settee, 'I can't say I know why *the world* as such, in general, or as a whole, but I do know why *we* are here and, moreover, why *you*, Mr. Tal, are here, assuming you really are here.'

'Why?' said Mr Tal.

The rentman suddenly looked unsure.

'Adolf,' said Painter.

'Hitler,' said Mr Tal, to himself.

Pause.

> 'Most of us, you see, never wanted to leave London; we all blamed Adolf Hitler.'

Pause.

Both Mr Tal and his head were now shaking. 'For my dear Stefan,' he said.

'You're here "For Stefan?"' I inquired.

Mr Tal nodded.

'And who's Stefan?' said Johanna.

'Our child,' whispered Mr Tal.

> In September 1939 Walter Benjamin's estranged wife Dora fled Nazi Germany for London with their son, Stefan, who initially stayed in Enfield Lock. Dora tried to persuade Benjamin to come with them but he refused.

'You have a child?' said Porlock. 'In that case,' he continued, 'I must ask you a few dozen questions. Please imagine, if you will, that I am the Assistant Medical Officer for Hertfordshire.'

'I think he *was* once,' said the rentman.

Porlock careered away and off into the house, straight and clean through the back door. And, after just a few seconds, he was knocking at that same door from the inside, crying, through the wood. 'Imagine,' he cried, 'that I, the Medical Officer, am at your door, your *front*-door.'

'Come in!' said the rentman.

No Medical Officer.

'Come in!' said the rentman.

Still no Medical Officer.

'Come, you bugger, come,' bellowed Painter.

This time Porlock did emerge, with a huge pencil and wooden clipboard. 'Why, thank you,' he said as he swept across the grass and leapt once more on his kitchen chair and stared down at Mr Tal. 'The following,' said Porlock, 'are just some of the devilish questions, riddles, and posers that are, even now, being put to the devilish folk of Utopia regarding their own dear, devilish infants.' He coughed and added, 'Are you ready?'

Mr Tal shook his head.

'Right – here goes,' said Porlock, who began to drop, from a very great height, his devilish questions; and, like Pilate, he did not wait for an answer. 'Has your child ever had pains in the joints?' he asked. 'Has your child ever had asthma?' he asked. 'Is his appetite poor?' he asked. 'Does he get frequent sore-throats?' he asked. 'And does a cold,' he asked, 'always go to his chest?' This last was a favourite.

After each question, Mr Tal shook his head; not to say 'No' but merely to indicate a refusal to answer. This did not seem to trouble Inquisitor Porlock. He was happy, if need be, to interrogate the trees, and so resumed his fearful quiz.

'Are you worried by the progress of your child at school?' he asked. 'Do you think he is a *nervous* child?' he asked. 'Does his behaviour worry you?' he asked. 'And has he been . . . ' (here the Inquisitor paused and looked hard at Mr Tal) ' . . . has he been separated from you for a month or more?' Porlock paused again. He enjoyed his work and would yet nail the Non Co-operator. 'Finally,' said Porlock, 'Does he . . . Does he . . . have . . . ' (he paused yet again) 'Does he have *nightmares*?'

'Bastard!' said Painter, and Mr Tal muttered something about 'That demonic fellow with the meter-long pencil.'

'I am sorry,' said Porlock, 'but the pencil cannot be helped.' He then looked up from his clipboard to see that Mr Tal had reclaimed his case and clutched it to his chest. Mr Tal made no other response to the Nightmare Question. Porlock tried again: 'Does he have nightmares?' Still Mr Tal said nothing. Porlock tried yet again: '*Does* he have nightmares?'

> On the Oxhey estate the number of children under the care of the Educational Psychologist and Child Guidance Clinic approached three times the usual percentage.

Mr Tal at last looked up. 'I lie in bed,' he said, 'and am disturbed by a child crying.'

'At last!' said Porlock. The medical demon smiled as he descended from the chair, saying, 'And where *is* this child? I should like to know.' Mr Tal looked around at the books that had fallen about him. Like so many embittered lovers, they were. In the end, he found the one he wanted, *A Directory of Dealers in Secondhand and Antiquarian Books in the British Isles, 1964–66.* Mr Tal hitched up his trousers again and searched through the book for a page he seemed to have in mind. He then handed the book to Porlock and pointed to one particular entry. Porlock read it aloud like a man condemned to enunciate each and every syllable: 'LIBRARY and SCIENTIFIC BOOK SUPPLY, 28 Museum Street, London WC1. Telephone: Bayswater 0525. Proprietor: –' (he paused) '– *Stefan Benjamin.*'

'Are you sure this is *your* Stefan?' asked Porlock, 'Your own and very Stefan? He whom you, far back in those Weimar days, once loved, once sang to, once played with, once dandled on your fine and Jewish knee?'

Mr Tal nodded.

'Why, then, do you not run to his arms?'

'I have hardly been out of my bed,' replied Mr Tal, 'and, hence, have been unable to activate my local contacts.'

'But the telephone?' inquired Porlock.

'There is no telephone in this apartment,' said Mr Tal, '– no telephone in this apartment.' He looked around at the garden.

'Can you not pay a visit?' inquired the rentman.

'I could probably make it to London sometime in January,' said Mr Tal.

'Yes,' said Porlock, 'you probably could, but I doubt that you will. Let us face one tyrannous fact: very few of us make it to London. It is true that we talk of going, but then there is either a crash, a terrible crash, or we miss the train distracted by a machine we must curse, or (quite simply) the soles fall right off of our shoes.'

'My feet,' said Painter, 'my feet are killing me.'

'And if we do make it,' continued Porlock, 'we no longer know how to live in the cracks of London and so, in the end, in the very end, we meekly hop-skip-and-jump-it all the way back. All the way back to Heaven.' Pause. 'Do we not?'

*West Herts and Watford Observer*
November 21, 1952

On Wednesday night a fourteen-year old boy was found shivering in a tent in Oxhey woods. He had lived on the estate until two months before, when his family returned to Shepherds Bush; but he had so missed the estate that he had runaway back to Oxhey.

*Grocery Van*

**Figure 7.1**
Mobile shop, Oxhey Estate, c 1948.
Here, a shop built like a tank, and mother is talking to mobile men.

## SCENE SEVEN

# STILL THE GARDEN IN THE EVENING

The woods, she thought, the woods out here grow crowded. Prodigals, who cannot go back, are in the woods, she thought. And, even as she thought, the wind dared to lift the fringe of her hair. She had dropped from the tree in the evening and began to write on the bark. Her knife was cruel.

*West Herts and Watford Observer*
November 13, 1953

> A sixteen-year old girl from the Oxhey estate appeared before Watford Juvenile Court; she was said to make up fantastic tales of where she had been and what she was doing. She was also said to associate with men who carried razors. Her father collapsed in court and her mother said she found her daughter to be pregnant.

I strained to see what it was she was writing. The initials of a lover, I thought. Or, an accuser. Or accused. But, no, it was more than a letter or two.

'The whore called "once upon a time,"' murmured Mr Tal.

As Johanna cut into the bark, I saw how thin and fine was her wrist, though scarred. I longed to touch Johanna and thought of putting my hand in her side, in the inward curve just above her hip. But Romeo, I thought, might be spying from the curtained room and he carried razors.

I mentioned the razors, and Painter folded, folded slowly to his knees in the clay while his hands still gripped the handle of the spade. The spade now propped him up.

'Help!' he cried.

No one moved.

'He prays,' said Porlock, balanced on the edge of a fragile wooden deckchair. He said he had borrowed it from an unsuspecting neighbour. Next to Porlock, on the ground, was a cup of tea. '*Cold* tea,' he said. 'Hence,' he said, 'this miracle of whiskey.' He waved a small bottle in his left hand. In his right, a thin Lucifer was wedged between two fingers.

'Help!' said Painter.

'It is a ruse,' said Porlock.

'Help!' said Painter.

'He calls for an angel,' said Porlock.

'Help!' said Painter.

I stepped toward him.

'Someone,' said Mr Tal, 'must be a fool if he is to help.'

I stopped dead.

'Only a fool's help,' said Mr Tal, 'is real help.'

I began to move again. But, by now, Porlock had thrown the cup of cold tea at Painter's face. The tea ran through the mud. Painter thanked God and heaved himself to his feet again; he then took his spade and began again to hurl the earth at his feet into the hole where his bicycle was slowly disappearing. All the while, he kept an eye on Johanna, who continued to knife the tree. His eye was bloodshot, and watered.

I watched her too, and thought about what it should be like, one night, to kiss, say, her lip or the nape of her neck, or even those eyelids when closed – so bruised, her sunset eyes. But soon she left, returning to the house.

'The only way of knowing a person,' said Mr Tal, 'is to love them without hope.'

'Hope of *what*?' said Painter.

'Hope,' said Porlock, 'of being the man' (he paused) '*in the house.*'

Mr Tal nodded. 'It is impotence,' he whispered, 'that makes for the Via Dolorosa.'

'Really?' said the rentman.

Mr Tal nodded again. 'The Via Dolorosa,' he said, 'of male sexuality.'

'Ooh, Nurse,' said the rentman, as if in pain.

'Draw the curtain,' added Porlock.

The pale comic refrain was complete. Their work was done. And the rentman was now a man profound. 'Surely, Mr. Tal,' he said, 'things can't be that bad. It's true we all like a bit of How's-Your-Father –'

Mr Tal said nothing.

'How's-Your-Father,' said the rentman.

Mr Tal said nothing.

'But if you can't, you can't,' said the rentman, 'No reason to crucify yourself.'

'Erotic motives,' whispered Mr Tal, 'may be at the bottom of suicide.' He then abandoned his heap of quotations, and, as he walked, a breeze blew, and they began, as if fallen leaves, to somersault away. Mr Tal was walking across the garden in the cool of the evening. Books were everywhere, and he stumbled over most like a clown at sea. But some, a few, he chose to save. 'Books and harlots,' he said, 'can be taken to bed.'

'Oh, just piss off!' said someone. It was Romeo. 'And take your bleeding library.' Another row of books threw themselves, as if broken hearted, from the upper room.

Mr Tal sat cross-legged on the grass, a Buddha among his books .

'Manna,' said Porlock, '. . . manna at dusk.' He blessed his bottle.

The sudden shower had, for the most part, ceased, but every now and then a belated book would land on Mr Tal's head or fall, wanton, into his lap, and whenever they did, he would abandon the volume he was reading and take up the newly beloved. He now surveyed the wreck all about him. 'I congratulate myself,' he whispered, 'on this archive.'

'But where?' said the rentman, 'Where did you get so many books?'

'From the library I left behind in Berlin,' said Mr Tal.

'Or perhaps,' said Porlock, 'from a first-floor window.'

'Or even,' said the rentman, 'from our own, very local and very public library. Five-hundred books, they say, are borrowed each and every week.'

'Though not all by a single Jew,' said Porlock, from the deckchair.

'Ah!' said the rentman. He stood corrected. He then paused to consider all that followed from this correction. Logically, as it were. He then spoke up: 'I see now, now at last, what they mean when they say, as they do, that us, us out here, we, together, all of us, we, together, have an incontinent thirst for books.'

'*Insatiable*,' said Porlock. He bent down to study the mechanics of the deckchair. Newtonian, thank God.

'I believe,' continued Porlock, 'we may be surrounded by many who read, many who smuggle out books they forever forget to return.'

*West Herts and Watford Observer*
January 19, 1950

Hertfordshire County Council has instituted a mobile library for the Oxhey estate. The library will make one to three visits each week and will house 27,000 books in a van 21 feet long, 11 feet high, and 7-and-a-half feet wide.

'Perhaps,' continued Porlock, 'Perhaps out here in Heaven we may yet amass, together, a whole stolen and clandestine library, one creviced in a thousand coal-scuttles.' Porlock struck a match, lit another devil and reclined.

'A nod,' said the rentman, 'is as good as a wink.' He winked.

'It is, you see,' continued Porlock, '– It is, you see, still possible that out hereabouts we shall not only read until our very eyes fall out but we shall think, learn, and think again and again, all until, all until, all until –' he waved his cigarette, 'all until –' (he paused) '– *Sweet Kingdom Come.*' The deckchair now collapsed, and with it Porlock. Newton wept.

Pause.

*Estate News*

December 1949

> Arrangements for adult education are forging steadily ahead. An Amateur Dramatic Society will begin in November, and every Tuesday there are already talks on Current Affairs. Also in hand are the formation of chess and draught clubs, a music-appreciation group, lessons in ballroom dancing, language classes, and talks on modern-day books.

'So, let us –,' said Porlock, he rose from the earth as if nothing had happened, bottle and cigarette still in hand, '– So, let us now get on and turn the leaves of our stolen books, each one heroically filched from this world's most precious library.'

'The Bibliothèque Nationale,' said Mr Tal, but was ignored.

'21 feet long, 11 feet high, and 7½ feet wide,' continued Porlock, '– these, Dear Inmates, are just three of the dimensions of our Ark, our strange and glorious Ark.'

Mr Nutt's boat-on-wheels passed by.

'And yet and yet,' said the rentman.

'And yet and yet *what?*' said Porlock. Now a hero in his cups.

The rentman pulled a ticket from the tree and read: 'Minutes of the Hertfordshire County Council Library Committee.'

A bird yawned, but the rentman carried on: '"It has been reported,"' he said, '"that the floor-covering in the mobile library has a dangerous tendency –."' Here the rentman paused.

'Yes?' said Porlock.

"– has a dangerous tendency, " continued the rentman, " . . . a dangerous tendency to –" (he paused again) "– *to pucker*" (the blow was struck).

Porlock winced. 'How can they be so sure?' he cried.

'My soles,' said Mr Tal, 'my soles would doubtless be the first to send me word.'

'True, so happily true,' said Porlock. 'But, come, come, let us lift our heavy eyes from library floor to library walls, walls that cradle all the books that have ever been sent to redeem us, You and I. For here, here, in the kitchens, gardens, and water-closets of Nowhere, we shall, my friends, read our way to –'

'Enfield?' asked the rentman.

'Why no!' said Porlock, '– New Jerusalem, New-New-Jerusalem.'

*West Herts and Watford Observer*
September 17, 1954

At their most recent meeting the Oxhey Estate Community Association were reminded by the Reverend Ron Williams that they should do 'Everything to strive for the intellectual, moral and educational development of the people on the estate.'

Porlock now lifted his bottle to the sunset, as if for God to drink. He then smoothed his hair and began, again, to make speeches to the evening winds. Slaughtered he was. 'Together,' he said, 'we shall forge –'

'Forge?' said the rentman.

'Yes, forge,' said Porlock, 'forge a literary history from within our very own rented space, a literary history that is pen-knifed upon our very own rented trees, and etched in our very own rented and yet radiant faces.'

I applauded, but Porlock had not finished. Slaughtered he was.

'And this history,' he declared, 'this history, it has a very particular grimace and gait, local habitation and name. Members and Members' Wives, I give you the incorrigible Maurice Carpenter.'

'Whom?' said the rentman.

'Come now,' said Porlock, 'All the People love Maurice Carpenter, otherwise known as Miles Carpenter – minor poet, major drinker, professional proletarian, Communist Party die-hard, friend (paradoxically) of Edith Sitwell, wearer of gawd-blimey trousers, and all-round sexual enthusiast.'

There was silence.

**Figure 7.1** Far left: Maurice Carpenter. London, July 2, 1948.

*Estate News*
August 1949

> The poet Maurice Carpenter has agreed to give a series of lecture-discussions on Modern Writers every Tuesday, beginning September 13, at 7.30 pm.

'What figure,' asked Mr Tal, 'does the writer cut when employed by the proletariat?'

'I am uncertain,' said Porlock.

'Meaning?' said the rentman.

'Meaning, I am not altogether certain,' said Porlock, 'that Mr. Carpenter ever actually turned up. We know he said he'd come, but we have no clear record, no hard evidence, that he did. It is just possible he didn't. Or perhaps, perhaps dear Maurice did make a show but we weren't there. Perhaps he turned up only to learn that out here there was no World to meet him, that we the People had something else on?'

'It being a Tuesday,' said the rentman.

*Minutes of the Hertfordshire Workers Education Association*
May 1958

> Is the initiative which drives people from London to the new towns of Hertfordshire the same kind of initiative that supports liberal education?

There was a silence. Then, all of a sudden, Porlock announced that the work of the poet W. H. Auden had once deeply affected him 'like –' (he paused to think) '– like a kick up the arse.'

'A lick?' said the rentman. He looked concerned.

'Please don't interrupt,' whispered Porlock, 'I am being Maurice Carpenter. Share the shabby illusion and allow me to play the part of Comrade Maurice employing nothing but his very own words, the devilish art of dissimulation, and not inconsiderable communion wine.' He tapped at his whiskey and swayed. 'Oh, and please be believing, if you will, that he, or "I," did indeed stroll by this way in 1952.'

'Right, fine, off you go!' said the rentman. He sat on the settee with a cup of tea, no saucer. Someone had left behind a copy of *The Daily Worker*. He picked it up.

'I, Maurice Carpenter,' began Porlock, 'minor poet, major drinker, Communist Party die-hard, and friend (paradoxically) of –'

'Edith Sitwell,' said the rentman. He didn't look up from *The Worker.*

'Good God! How did you know?' asked Porlock-cum-Carpenter.

'Grace,' said the rentman.

'Damn!' said Porlock, who swayed again.

'Four sheets,' said Painter, 'he's four sheets to the wind.'

Pause.

'I, Maurice Carpenter,' said Porlock, 'was born in 1911 on September 25.'

Mr Tal twitched then stretched himself out on the grass. But Porlock-cum-Carpenter went on: 'My alter ego, "*Miles* Carpenter," however, was born when two black-shirted darlings of Sir Oswald Mosley walloped a young "*Maurice* Carpenter" over the cranium with his own bleeding bugle after an anti-fascist knees-up on the forsaken steps of Hammersmith Town Hall.'

'Blessed days,' said the rentman.

'The journalist,' said Carpenter, 'who reported the incident had, you see, an impediment which meant he mispronounced "Maurice" as "Miles."'

'Marvellous,' said the rentman. He looked at a photograph of a football team. Moscow Dynamo FC. All of England they would tour. Muscular excellence and teamwork.

'I was, you must understand, a walking protest against the world,' said Carpenter.

'Still more marvellous,' said the rentman. He examined the photograph of a bathing beauty in Leningrad. How she stared.

'In the Dirty Thirties,' continued Carpenter, 'I cleaved to the Party in the manner of an unwashed vest, and wandered lost in Archers Bookshop, Red Lion Square. Poetry, politics, and piss-heads.'

'Very nice,' said the rentman, although he thought she looked rather cold.

'But what,' said Carpenter, 'what I really wanted –'

'Yes?' inquired the rentman.

'– was a fuck.'

The rentman dropped his cup of tea, no saucer, and it fell to his lap as he danced to his feet in an attempt to calm the scalded crutch of his outraged trousers.

'Yes,' said Carpenter, very solemn, 'All I needed was a fuck.'

'You quote?' asked the rentman, now down on all fours as he tried, in vain, to make good his cup of tea.

'Yes, yes,' said Carpenter, 'from my very own autobiography.'

'Fair enough' said the rentman, 'And may I inquire, just for the minutes, whether you ever did get your brush up the chimney?'

The minor poet thought hard – as hard, he said, as a poet could or even should. 'Mary Rose,' he finally said, 'Yes, Mary Rose. She made a living from purveying her perfumed body along Hammersmith Broadway, and yet, kind girl, was prepared to oblige local Comrades for free.'

'Where?' asked the rentman. He reached for his ledger.

'On the settee,' said Carpenter, 'in the front room, her mother popping in from time to time to look on, benign.'

'And all for free!' said the rentman.

'An outstanding female Communist,' said Mr Tal.

We applauded. Carpenter then remembered he was a poet, albeit minor, and bent to pick from the earth a single book.

'The Ballad of John Nameless,' he said. 'By me,' he said. And off he went: 'Where are you England?' he began, 'Where are you Labouring England?'

'Search me,' shouted the rentman. He had popped to the toilet.

'Steeped in a dream of an England for all,' continued Carpenter, 'They shall never go down to the shadows forgotten.'

'I think they have,' shouted the rentman. He pulled the flush.

'While there are fighters to follow their trail,' concluded Carpenter.

'Doesn't rhyme,' said Painter.

'*Minor* poet,' said the rentman, beside us once more.

'But all I wanted,' insisted Carpenter, 'was a fuck.'

'I know,' murmured Painter, 'I know.' He stared at his feet.

'Just a fuck,' said Carpenter.

'Not my Department,' said the rentman.

('Nor hers,' whispered Porlock, for a moment he was not Comrade Carpenter. He gestured towards the house, towards Johanna. 'Not for the duration,' he added.)

Pause. Pause.

'*We* . . . ,' announced Carpenter, '*We* . . . ,' he said again, '*We* are midwives of a queer nativity.'

'*How* queer?' inquired the rentman, returning to the settee.

Carpenter looked unsure, but then he seemed to remember. 'The trouble in the street enters the bar,' he said, 'A Jew, dishevelled, enters to a flutter of handkerchiefs.'

The rentman pointed out that, sadly, our very own dishevelled Jew had, some minutes ago, quite nodded off. Carpenter hadn't noticed, but now he joined Painter, his shovel and myself, as there we stood way above Mr Tal who, still horizontal, had begun to snore. Carpenter looked down at Mr Tal and whispered, 'All good poets die young.' The rentman said he thought that, in point of fact, Mr Tal was not in the dying way but was simply enjoying forty winks. Carpenter shook his head. 'The time he lived in,' he said, 'made the kind of poet he was impossible.' Painter threw a shovel of earth all over Mr Tal.

'Like K. in *The Trial*,' continued Carpenter, 'he has reached a threshold he cannot cross.' Painter threw another shovel of earth at Mr Tal.

'But perhaps . . . ,' said Carpenter. Painter held back, at the very last moment, from throwing still more of the earth.

'But perhaps,' said Carpenter, 'he found the means to tunnel *beneath* the door.'

Painter threw away his shovel, and gave Mr Tal an almighty kick. There was hope, I thought, and peered, looking to see if Mr Tal would move, would respond, but he couldn't, couldn't tunnel beneath the door.

'The singer,' said Carpenter, 'is sleeping. His head is on the cold rail.'

'It has to be somewhere,' observed the rentman.

'Anchored,' said Carpenter, 'Anchored to agony, he awaits the breath –'

'The breath?' said the rentman, from the settee.

'Yes, the breath,' insisted Carpenter.

'The breath of *what*?' asked the rentman.

'The breath,' said Carpenter, 'of *the snake train!*'

> ' . . . I once saw a suicide victim on the railway line . . . he had thrown himself from the platform and gone right under the train. The heels of his

> shoes had been perfectly detached from his soles and lay about thirty yards away. . . .'

Painter kicked again at Mr Tal, but still he did not move.

'Your writhing,' said Carpenter, 'cannot rouse him. He is congealed on the dead tree.'

'Bollocks,' said Painter. He kicked Mr Tal where it hurts. Always.

'And your priestess, Eurydice . . . ,' began Carpenter, he glanced at the house, 'She reaches to him from the companion cross on the left.'

'Bollocks,' said Painter.

'Whilst on the right . . . ,' said Carpenter, he stared at Painter, 'Writhes Prometheus of the Poor, eaten by eagles.'

Painter now seized Maurice Carpenter by the very ears. 'Mr. Minor Poet,' he said, 'just tell us this: Did you or did you not come our way?'

The Minor Poet had not a clue.

'Tuesdays,' said Painter, 'You were supposed to come on Tuesdays.'

The Poet still had not the faintest. 'All I wanted was a fuck,' he said.

'No!' howled Painter. 'No!' For a moment he did not move. I thought Painter might cleave and splinter. He did not. He simply shook his head, and began again, back at the Beginning.

'Just answer my question,' he said. '*Did* you come to see us? Were we there? What find? What see? What? What?'

Carpenter paused, then at last responded. 'I failed,' he announced, looking straight at Painter, 'I failed to find a mature, independent, and cultured working-class.'

'Still quoting?' asked the rentman.

'Naturally,' said Carpenter.

'Just checking,' said the rentman.

'Bastard,' said Painter, who now let go of both Carpenter and his ears.

'But this cultured working-class,' resumed Carpenter, 'just did not exist. I did once think it could be created,' he said, his face into the sun, '*But*,' (he whispered) 'our society' (he whispered) 'has not developed' (he whispered) 'as Marx had predicted.' With this, Maurice Carpenter waved his arms in the direction of a hundred abandoned evenings.

> *Her Majesty's Inspectors' Survey*
> *of Further Education* 1954
>
> The following courses were announced to run on the Oxhey estate but failed to start for lack of numbers: Local History, German, Choral Singing, Book-binding, English Literature, and Household Repairs.

Silence. And in the silence Mr Tal awoke, and sat up. 'The masses,' he whispered, 'do not wish to be instructed.' He paused. 'Their education is a series of catastrophes that befall them at fairs.'

'At fairs?' said the rentman. He was impressed.

But Mr Tal, still sat on the grass, was already somewhere else. 'Brecht,' he said, 'found me in the garden reading *Das* –.'

'Please,' begged Porlock (he had now given up being Carpenter) '– please, no more Brecht-in-the-Garden.' Porlock looked all around. 'And, please, no more *Das Cap-It-All*.' He tickled his bottle and swayed. 'For we have seen it all, you know.' He swayed. 'And need no lessons in revolution, you know.' He swayed. 'Out around here' (he swayed again) 'we *ourselves* shall re-make the world.' Sway.

'Just the world?' inquired the rentman.

'We shall –,' Porlock went on, 'We shall remake the world out of English –'

He hesitated.

'Lampshades?' asked the rentman.

'No,' said Porlock. If only he could remember whatever it was.

'Wicker-baskets?' asked the rentman, trying again.

'No,' said Porlock, very sadly.

'Soil?' said the rentman. Inspired.

'Yes!' said Porlock. 'Out here we shall remake the world from English *soil*!'

*Estate News*
May 1949

> 'Now Spring is here, life is stirring in the ground, and the gardens are beginning to augur well for the future and herald a new life.' (Editor)

Painter was about to speak, from by the window, the kitchen window, where he now stood and looked back into the house. 'You know that Arse from the British Legion,' he said, 'the Arse with the nose, the big one?'

'Nose?' inquired Porlock.

'Arse,' said Painter, without turning around.

'And what of Arse?' said Porlock.

'Arse,' said Painter, 'Arse says to me, he says, "You on the estate, you have no traditions."'

'Arse is a Tit,' said the rentman.

'But you know *what*?' said Painter, as if to the window.

'What?' said the rentman.

'Arse is right,' said Painter.

'Arse always is,' said the rentman, now wrestling the standard lamp.

'But what Arse don't know,' said Painter, 'is that we don't want no bloody traditions.'

'No, no – don't blooming want them,' said the rentman, now trying to straighten the shade.

'Out here,' said Painter, 'we don't hang around remembering.' He still faced the window.

'No. No remembering here,' said the rentman. 'Just hanging around,' he said, as the shade fell off.

*Estate News*
May 1949

> 'Let those who would weep now dry their eyes and face the change. History has little time for side-shows.' (Editor)

Pause.

Mr Tal rose from the ground and slouched towards the settee. 'I am,' he said, 'close to tears.' He sat himself down, hard by the rentman.

The rentman offered Mr Tal a well-folded handkerchief. 'There-there,' said the rentman, 'things can't be all that bad. You may have lost your child, your books, your –'

'Life,' said Porlock.

'Such as it was,' added the rentman. 'But, but, look on the Funny Side,' he went on. 'That's what we do out here in Heaven – we have a good old laugh, hell of a laugh.'

'A welter of abortions,' said Mr Tal.

'Come again?' said the rentman.

'Abortions,' said Mr Tal, 'abortions.'

Pause.

'Look,' said the rentman, 'This'll make you howl.' He rose, picked up the tray and waltzed off to the other side of the garden. There, over there, the sun was beginning to fall. Straight through the floor of the horizon. Once the rentman had reached the garden's far side, he waved like one who was miles away; he then turned and walked straight towards Mr Tal. The rentman looked as if he was about to offer Mr Tal a cup of tea from his tray, but just as the rentman approached Mr Tal, he pretended to trip and, for an instant, it looked like all of English slap-stick, every last teacup, every last slap and stick, was about to descend on Mr Tal. But no, he was, said Painter, just pissing the world around.

'The comic figure,' said Mr Tal wearily, 'stumbles over his own feet.'

'Got to stumble over something,' observed the rentman.

'The clowning of despair,' said Mr Tal.

Pause.

'The comic figure –' said Mr Tal.

'Yes?' said the rentman.

'The comic figure,' said Mr Tal, 'is the only angel suited to this world.'

'Bless you,' said the rentman, then adding: 'Behold, a funny walk!' He threw the whole bloody tray right over his shoulder. Almighty great crash. He then stood on one leg, his right one, thin-thin-thin, and he bent it at the same time as he stuck out his other one, his left, but just as thin, as far as ever he dare.

'If,' said Mr Tal, 'one had to expand the doctrine of antiquity while standing on one leg . . . '

'To be honest,' said the rentman, 'I was thinking of a pratfall.' He was just about to demonstrate when Painter reminded him that history had no time for sideshows.

'Not even a bring-and-buy sale?' said the rentman.

Silence.

'Sale of work?' said the rentman.

Silence.

'Bric-a-brac stall?' said the rentman.

Silence.

> ' . . . The big event of each year, for us in the Party, was the *The Daily Worker* bazaar where we raised funds. It was, though, so tiring to set up and run we would joke that we could never plan a revolution at the same time as the bazaar. . . .'

'Bloody sideshows,' said Painter.

'For which – but don't tell me,' said the rentman, 'history has no time. I know.' He was limbering up for another comic walk, he said. And on this occasion there would be hopping. He was doing his bit, he said, for the Revolution.

'I,' said Mr Tal, 'was born under the planet of *slow* revolution.'

'I think,' whispered the rentman, 'he's got the wrong end of the stick.'

'Stick?' said Porlock, now leaning against the tree.

There was a pause while the rentman seemed to put his mind to all of this. Mr Tal then returned to that planet of his.

'The star of hesitation and delay,' he said.

'Well, you'll love it here, then,' said the rentman.

'Quite so,' said Porlock, who slid his whiskey into one pocket, and from another drew out a paper. A fair exchange. And began to read aloud, for the edification of all: "*WestHerts and Watford Observer*, April 20, 1951," he began. "On Saturday last, representatives of the Oxhey LCC Community Association –"

'Bolsheviks,' said the rentman, once more with Mr Tal, on the settee.

'"– met with the County Education Committee."'

'Fascists,' said the rentman.

'"– to discuss problems with hiring out the new school hall."'

'Glass all over. Modern, very modern,' said the rentman.

'"It was, therefore, somewhat ironical."'

'Ironical?' said the rentman.

'Yes, ironical,' said Porlock, '"ironical that the deputation had to wait outside the school, for fifteen minutes, in the rain."'

Pause. Porlock returned the paper to the innards of his jacket.

'Humanity,' said Mr Tal, 'is *born* from the spirit of irony.'

'Born?' said Painter. He tapped at the kitchen window. No answer. 'Born?' he said again.

> Walter Benjamin's death was a deeply ironic affair, an uncommon stroke of bad luck. The day *before* he reached Port Bou the border had been open; and a day *later* his companions were allowed through. Only on that particular day was the catastrophe possible.

'He who lives by irony,' said Porlock, 'shall die by –'

'Wednesday?' said the rentman.

'No – *Friday*,' said Porlock, tapping at the bark of the tree.

Pause. Johanna reappeared, hands cut off at the wrist by the pockets of her skirt.

'Irony,' muttered Mr Tal, 'Irony, false mistress.' He looked across at Johanna who touched the short dark fury of her hair and stretched high her arms as if feeling for the sky. She glanced up at Romeo's shadow. It winked and, for a moment, disappeared before returning somewhere behind a mattress that slowly squeezed itself through the open window. The mattress, a single affair, for such as lie alone, had a weary air, as if quite exhausted by sleep, and fell through the sunset to the ground beneath and there flop-flopped to end, kneeling, at the shoes of Mr Tal. A gift, he thought, and slid from the settee to the mattress.

'Very nonchalant,' observed the rentman.

'If you knew,' said Mr Tal, 'how bad the worst mattress in the world is . . . '

'We all,' said the rentman, 'have our cross to bear.'

'I have hardly been out of my bed,' continued Mr Tal.

'Enough of your pissing bed,' cried Romeo, 'Just bugger off.'

Mr Tal made himself comfortable on the mattress.

'And these,' cried Romeo, 'these can bugger off *with* you.' He let fly hundreds of letters; each one, a falling bird made of the thinnest of paper, slowly felt its way to earth.

Painter now left his post at the window, knelt down and began to read, aloud, each one: 'Dearest Dora . . . Love Walter,' 'My Dear Walter . . . Yours for ever, Dora'; and so on, time and again, ever and again, yours ever and again. And, as the sky dropped about our ears, so the letters whispered the clumsy music of a clumsy marriage.

'And where,' said Porlock, he turned to Mr Tal, 'where did you *find* these here letters?'

Mr Tal didn't answer. Not minded to say. All he would offer was, 'Dora has opened up a boarding-house in London.' He shuttered his eyes. No vacancies. And there he lay on the weary mattress with both hands lost to the pockets of his trousers, and two feet crossed; like a clerk, from an office, stretched, recumbent, in his lunch hour, on the perfect grass of the Tiergarten. Of the letters, he was, though, still silent.

> Soon after Stefan Benjamin's death the entire correspondence between Dora and Walter Benjamin was stolen from Stefan's house in Hampstead, North-West London. These letters have never been found.

Mr Tal opened a spinning eye. 'The house,' he said, 'had been burglarized.'

'The house full of letters?' asked Porlock, forsaking the tree.

No answer.

'The house in Hampstead?' asked Porlock.

Mr Tal sat up and pointed at Painter. 'The proletariat,' he said, 'has the appearance of planning a burglary.'

'That is as may be,' replied Porlock, 'but you, dear madman, have the air of having actually *effected* one. Stolen letters needs must go somewhere, must crawl into someone's empty pocket, seep into someone's empty attic.' Porlock took a spoon from his pocket and tapped it twice, hard, on the top of Mr Tal's skull.

'For my dear *Stefan*,' said Mr Tal.

'No! "*From* your dear Stefan!"' said Porlock, as if Sherlock himself. 'I say that you stole these books and letters from the man you call your son.'

'Blimey,' said the rentman.

Mr Tal lay down again, turned heavily on to his side, and murmured: 'If you knew how bad the worst mattress in the world is . . . .'

Silence. Then Johanna, that girl, she whispered. 'I *do*,' she whispered, 'I *do* know how bad is the worst.' She lowered and lay herself, still, beside Mr Tal. She then moved, turning her body towards him and setting his hand on her thigh. Five ink-cured fingers. Mr Tal felt the warmth of the flesh she had offered and moved his hand. North and inland. Mr Tal then stopped, at a border, repelled his own advance and threw his body away. 'It is impotence,' said Mr Tal, 'it is impotence that makes for the Via Dolorosa.'

Time it was, they said, for Johnny Homeless to be going home.

Daily Mirror

FRI FEB 7 1958

2½d FORWARD WITH THE PEOPLE No. 16,843

# SOCCER AIR TRAGEDY

## Manchester United plane crashes

## 21 dead

**THE END** The chartered Elizabethan airliner in which the Manchester United team was travelling home lies shattered in a snowfield near Munich. The pilot, Captain James Thain, escaped alive from the smashed nose

**THE BEGINNING** This picture was taken when the team, accompanied by sports writers, boarded the plane at Manchester on Monday. Left to right, with known survivors marked with asterisk*: Jackie Blanchflower* Billy Foulkes* Walter Crickmer, secretary; Don Davies, Manchester Guardian; Roger Byrne, captain; Duncan Edwards*, Albert Scanlon* — just visible behind Scanlon is Frank Swift, News of the World; Ray Wood*; Dennis Viollet*; Archie Ledbrooke, Daily Mirror; Geoff Bent; Mark Jones and Alf Clarke, Kemsley Newspapers.

AN Elizabethan airliner—on charter to Manchester United football team, the fabulous "Busby Babes"—crashed on take-off at Munich Airport, Germany, yesterday, and plunged the world of Soccer into mourning.

Twenty-one men — among them some of the brightest stars in British football—died.

Seven Manchester United players who died were:

Roger Byrne (Capt.), Tommy Taylor, Mark Jones, Eddie Colman, Billy Whelan, David Pegg, Geoff Bent.

Also dead was ex-England goalkeeper and sports writer Frank Swift.

In hospital, fighting for his life, was manager Matt Busby.

Not far from him ace centre half Jackie Blanchflower lay with a broken pelvis.

Twenty-three of the 44 passengers survived.

Among the dead was Archie Ledbrooke, the Mirror's famous Northern sports writer. His last story is on Page 21.

- THE CRASH—Story and pictures Back Page and Page 5.
- THE TEAM in the Tragedy—See Centre Pages.

—Blackest Day of All—By Peter Wilson —See Page 23—

**Figure 8.1** The Munich Air Disaster, 1958.

## SCENE EIGHT

# THE GARDEN, NOW FROZEN, AT NIGHT

The summer evening was, at last, a winter's night, and the garden all frozen. Near the back door, and by a single kitchen chair, Painter's packing case had reappeared; once more it was on its head, although now it bore up a delicate Victorian sewing machine. By the tree stood a stray foldaway chair and table, a felt-topped table designed for the playing of whist. On it sat an ancient typewriter. Little Moscow was cold, and so was I.

'You have,' said Mr Tal, 'no wish to leave this cave.'

'No wish,' I said.

I looked back at the house, to a room that was lit by a black-and-white screen with a storm of a thousand tiny, fizzing, dots, each finely shaded. My eyes were fixed on this electric storm and, in the middle of it all, a single man. A pale and elegant figure he was, a strolling player in a foreign and floodlit field.

> 'Everyone on the estate, it seemed, loved football. In fact, it was the *only* game. As children we played it all the time and, on the rare occasion it was screened, we would watch it flicker on the television.'

It was hard to see into the room, what with the frost all over the window from the terrible cold and, behind me, a garden lit by three huge light bulbs that were each reflected in the glass. But I wanted so much to watch the faraway player. I screwed up my eyes and peered as hard as ever I could.

Mr Tal paid no heed, being busy at the typewriter, laying upon it the heaviest of hands. He wore gloves with holes at the ends of the fingers and spoke as he typed, as if dictating, his breath, spiralling, visible in the air. He was composing, he said, 'The Metaphysics of Youth,' and the lightless estate fell finally to its sleep as the essay began with the words (he spoke aloud) 'Our glances meet.' Through the glass and in the glass I saw the footballer stroll, jog and then, for an instant, make as if to run. 'The dance now begins,' said Mr Tal. And he rose to his feet, forsook his writing machine and began to dance, slowly, with an invisible beauty. As he danced, so he continued to dictate, even though there was no one there to type. 'We do not arouse each other from our dreams,' he gently promised the air.

> 'Most people supported the big London clubs, like Arsenal or Spurs, but for me, and many others, the most glamorous was Manchester United, the first English champions of Europe – that was 1968, exactly ten years after they had lost eight brilliant young players in the Munich air crash. Everyone was affected by the Munich Disaster.'

The distracted player seemed to sleepwalk, as if seeing a hundred other games he had played in the past, a hundred dead passes, runs, turns, feints and falls. Slow motion.

'Our bodies make careful contact,' sighed Mr Tal, continuing, in the cold, his enchanted waltz.

'Munich,' said Painter. He had joined me before the window, no less drawn to the floodlit field and its four great suns.

'How we love each other!' declared Mr Tal, turning elegantly.

'February 6, 1958,' said Painter. He shivered.

The footballer was edged by four long shadows.

'We are in a house without windows, a ballroom without world,' said Mr Tal.

'BEA Flight 609,' said Painter, pulling tight the collar-and-soul of his coat.

I wanted so much to be that distant player, as he raised and spread wide his arms to point, to direct, to accuse, to beckon, to appeal, to plead, to beseech, to protest.

'We hurl ourselves into the rhythm of the violins,' cried Mr Tal, attempting to leap into the air.

'Ice on the runway,' said Painter, scratching the frost on the window.

The player leaps, stops, swerves, deceives, wipes sweat from his brow and clasps the head now in his hands.

'Never was a night more ethereal, more uncanny, more chaste,' announced Mr Tal, arching his spine.

'Three times,' said Painter, 'three times they tried. Tried to take off.' I sensed that Mr Tal's waltz was approaching its end and that, alas, his exquisite partner would have to take her leave. 'Our hands slide off one another,' lamented Mr Tal. The floodlit player, now bowed, bends towards the pitch, those hands on his hips. 'Twenty-one dead,' said Painter, turning from the glass. Appalled. He trudged towards the light bulbs, in the far corner of the garden. The bulbs were his. He had bought them.

Pause.

Pause.

At last the dance was over, the waltz was done and Mr Tal, looking through the glass at my chosen player, my player of players, slowly whispered, 'The thinker, the loiterer, the *flâneur*, the dreamer, the ecstatic.'

'Yes,' I said, not knowing what he meant.

'In Paris,' he continued, 'a football stadium, the Stade Columbe, was selected as an assembly camp for refugees from Germany.' He said he had been there, had been held there. Ten days and nights.

Mr Tal then turned back to the garden, climbed onto the settee, still with that burden, his case, and waved his free arm. 'We stand,' he cried, 'on a cartload of fantasies, alone in the bright night of nights which *we* conjured up.' Mr Tal looked unutterably proud of Painter's three light bulbs, this hint of footlights, rumour of music hall. Then, in an instant, Mr Tal leapt from the settee with all the élan of a suicide. 'Our fleeing soul,' he said, as he landed, 'invites a woman to come – a girl who stands at the end of a distant room.'

I looked again at the room lit by the television, but could nowhere see either woman or girl. I then turned back to the cold garden and spied Johanna. She wore a dressing gown of stolen silk, and beneath I could see to the pale of her thigh. Astonished, I walked towards the garden swing, its cold iron frame, the wooden seat and the metal chains from which it hung, all frosted, and there I sat and began to swing. And, as I kicked the night air, I thought of the shivering beauty of Leningrad, and Johanna drew the gown more tightly about her waist.

'She walks regally,' said Mr Tal, 'across the parquet floor that lies so smoothly between the dancers.' Johanna paused for a moment as if to resist a hypnotist. She then sat down by the upturned packing case, on which stood the sewing machine. It was a Singer machine, sing-sing. Bending her head low, she began, as if to keep warm, to turn and to turn again and again the beautiful handle. Cold labour, sing-sing. So cold she was, this cold-cold nightingale.

*Estate News*

January 1950

The dressmaking classes are proceeding well; though, much to our regret, the County Education Authorities do not provide sewing machines. They have, however, promised sufficient machines by

> November to enable the ladies to assemble the garments they have cut out.

Mr Tal looked across at Johanna, but continued to talk of the girl at the end of a distant room. 'Her stately step,' he cried, 'creates order among the dancers –'

'Sweet Jesus,' whispered Porlock.

'– where,' continued Mr Tal, 'people move along corridors, as if on tightropes through the night.' I looked up from my swing, my pendulum, looking for tightropes, but could see only frost-white telephone wires. No acrobats, none, all gone. Mr Tal would not, though, be stopped. 'When,' he asked, '– when did night ever attain brightness and become radiant, if not here?' Again he looked across at Painter's lights and smiled as if these were the very Illuminations of Blackpool.

*West Herts and Watford Observer*
January 23, 1948

> At Watford Magistrates Court Mr. Arthur L. Thomas was charged with breaking and entering an equipment store on the new LCC Oxhey housing estate. He was accused of stealing 875 yards of electric cable and 475 switches.

'Out here,' said Porlock, 'we may have no street-lights –'

'No streets,' observed the rentman. Acute. No flies on him, no flies; he, who had just escaped from the house. Back door. The kitchen.

'Nevertheless, and notwithstanding,' continued Porlock, 'we do have all the electricity we could ever desire; sufficient, dare I say it, even to power this here Almighty Great Wireless.' This machine of interference, this whopping great box, was right there, in the garden, as if someone had just dreamed it. Porlock switched it on and the box wept a song of sorts, and crackled. Interference.

'The music,' said Mr Tal, 'transports our thoughts surrounded by the flowing night.' He began, once again, to dance (one-two-three, one-two-three), but this time as if he were most terribly sad and could only remember. Berlin. One-two-three, one-two-three. Berlin.

'*And*,' he murmured, 'to the strains of a Viennese waltz beneath the very bridges on whose parapet one leaned in summer . . . ' – his voice faded, but on and on he waltzed alone across the whitening grass. On and on. Then, quick as sin, the music stopped. (Porlock's intervention.) And so did Mr Tal. Scared he was. Witless. 'But!' he cried, 'We *know*,' he put his hands to his head, 'We *know* that all the merciless realities that have been expelled still flutter round this house.' He looked around, hunting for realities.

'The poets,' he said, 'the poets with their bitter smiles.' He looked up at the bedroom window. 'And the saints,' he said, 'and the policemen, and the waiting cars.'

'Ah!' said Porlock, '– our brave policemen.' He tapped the huge radiogram.

'The house,' said Mr Tal, 'surrounded by unparalleled darkness, by horror and incest –'

'Incense?' said the rentman, 'I don't approve of incense.'

'*Incest*,' said Mr Tal, '*incest*.'

'Oh, that's all right,' said the rentman. He glanced at Painter.

Pause. Mr Tal sat down, on the cold-cold grass. Pause.

'A situation,' said Mr Tal, 'with no escape.'

'A situation?' asked the rentman, for the record.

'A situation,' confirmed Mr Tal.

'With no escape?' asked the rentman, again for the minutes.

'With no escape,' confirmed Mr Tal.

'Sounds more like a *predicament*,' said the rentman.

Mr Tal, still sat on the grass, was beaten. 'A situation with no escape,' he insisted. He then spoke again, as if he wanted to end the world and this would be the very last word: '*Surrounded*,' he said.

Pause.

'These Londoners,' said Mr Tal, 'their police have tanks.'

'Indeed,' said Porlock, 'thousands of them. But then, the Fifth Column must be dealt with.'

At that moment, a young man, half-clad, dashed through the darkest part of the garden, just behind the freezing tree. 'A lover,' said Mr Tal, 'slips through the night.'

'Romeo,' observed Porlock.

'Unmasking others,' said Mr Tal.

'The boy cannot help it,' said Porlock, 'He moves in the most terrible circles: the poets, the saints, the police.'

Mr Tal nodded. 'There are spies,' he shouted, '– spies everywhere.'

'Quiet!' said the rentman, 'Quiet!'

'Do you not want me,' asked Mr Tal, 'to hang the red flag from my window?'

'No, not the red flag,' said Porlock. He didn't think that was a good idea.

'Nor a filthy mattress,' said Johanna, half to herself.

'You *must* understand, Herr Tal,' said Porlock, '– the house really *is* surrounded.'

> ' . . . Because my father was so involved in the Communist Party they tapped our telephone (we were one of the first on the estate to get one). It went on for years and became a running joke, just a fact of life. Goodness knows what they thought they were going to hear. . . .'

Mr Tal, still low on the grass, now spoke to the dark. 'Dear Invisible Listeners,' he said. His voice had turned black as if he wanted revenge and was ready, at last, to turn against all the shadows that pursued him, and now, at last, knew exactly how he would do so. 'The policemen, the waiting cars,' he said, '– from time to time, *music*' (he pounced on the word) 'submerges them!' Mr Tal jumped to his feet.

'I beg your coupon?' said the rentman.

'Music,' said Mr Tal, 'Music submerges them!' He clumsily punched the air, his small fleshy hand clenched tight.

'Submerges *who*?' asked Porlock.

'The police, the waiting cars,' said Mr Tal.

'Oh, I shouldn't think they mind a little music,' said Porlock. But Painter, busy with his lights, in the far corner of the garden, seemed to like the idea: 'Right!' he said, 'Crank up the gram and blast to hell all who –'

'Who *what*?' inquired the rentman.

'Why, all who *listen in on us*,' said Porlock.

Pause.

Mr Tal retreated to the stray table-and-chair, hard by the tree, and began to examine his now-whitened quotations. Porlock sank into his deckchair. This, his borrowed throne, was within a yard of the radiogram, and had been somehow rebuilt with string and with hope. As before, he managed both a cigarette and a small bottle. 'Liberty Hall!' he cried. He then looked at the stars as if, even after all these days out here, they still surprised him.

'Bugger liberty,' said Painter. 'Turn your wireless on and let them have it.'

Porlock, juggling more than ever, cigarette-bottle, bottle-cigarette, leaned across to the radiogram, a perilous operation, and, reaching out, turned the huge dial, sweeping through a hundred nocturnal frequencies.

'Any chance of *ITMA*?' said the rentman.

ITMA, (*It's That Man Again*), the BBC radio comedy, ran from 1939 to 1949 and starred Tommy Handley along with a host of absurdly-named characters and a hundred catchphrases. The title was a contemporary phrase referring to ever-more frequent news-stories about Adolf Hitler in the months and weeks before World War II.

'Louder!' said Painter.

'Ali Oop, Mona Lott, Mrs. Mopp,' said the man from *ITMA*, '– kill me, they do.'

Porlock turned up the volume. He was now, quite suddenly, 'All for hue and cry' and, getting to his feet, waved his bottle at the cold and the noise and swayed and yelled. 'Hear!' he cried, 'Hear the howl of Nowhere!' (sway). 'Yes, and even . . . Yes and even,' (sway), '– the crash of sweet Utopia!'

'"Can I do you now, Sir?"' asked Mrs Mopp.

'No,' said Porlock. 'Be gone.' He pointed at the dark.

'He *died*, mind you,' (it was that rentman again) '– Tommy Handley, his brain, just like that. Hemorrhage it was. Bloody hemorrhage.'

Pause.

'Listen!' said Porlock. Skeletal hand to his ear.

Silence.

'Listen!' said Porlock. Hand-ear, ear-hand.

Silence.

'*That*,' said Porlock, now pointing at the silence, '*That* is the sound of fourteen thousand angels all calling committees, taking minutes, planning paradise, and –' (he was by now addressing the deckchair) '– and yes, finally, finally, re-wiring Utopia.' Porlock threw apart his thin brown arms, like Jesus, his cigarette lost as his arms went flying. He then offered his bottle to the rentman.

'"Don't mind if I do!"' said That Man Yet Again.

'Fourteen thousand *angles*,' said Porlock, he struggled with drunken words, '475 swishes and 875 years of cabable. . . .' He then pulled himself together, with string, and said: 'Utopia, you see, has been re-wired as a huge great *bomb*.'

Mr Tal nodded. 'Truth,' he said, 'wants to be startled abruptly from her self-immersion.'

'She does?' said the rentman.

Mr Tal nodded. 'Startled by uproar,' he insisted.

'Uproar?' said Porlock. He swayed to the North, then steadied himself to wrench again the huge dial. In search he was of Uproar and that startled girl 'Truth.' For a while, the misfiring wireless battered the garden; but if 'Truth' were sweet Johanna she wasn't to be startled. Nothing could startle her. Not any more.

The wireless failed again.

'Bloody wireless,' said Painter, leaving his lights. He gave the radio an almighty great kick. 'The air's not ours,' he said. 'Them buggers at the BBC, it's their bloody air, and they run every bloody show – even this one.' He pointed at Utopia. 'Lord Bloody Reith,' he cursed.

> In September 1945 Lord Reith, former Director General of the BBC, chaired the committee set up to consider 'the promotion of new towns in furtherance of the policy of planned decentralization from congested urban areas.'

'Exactly!' cried Porlock, 'Welcome to The Lord Reith Overspill Show. Time, gentlemen, to go On Air.' He swayed to the South, but this time could not steady the ship and fell backwards towards the deckchair. 'Air,' he said as he fell, '– time to go On Air.'

Mr Tal seemed to have heard these words before. In an instant, he settled himself at the table-and-chair, moved the typewriter to one side, shuffled a pack of papers and prepared to speak into a spectral microphone.

> It is a fact often overlooked that, from 1929 to 1933, Walter Benjamin wrote and broadcast at least thirty radio-talks. Each one was a talk for children.

'Dear Invisible Listeners,' said Mr Tal. He stared into the cold. 'I feel,' he said, 'like a chemist when I talk to you over the radio.'

'I beg your gas-mask?' said the rentman.

'My weights,' continued the man at the microphone, 'are the minutes, and I have to measure them accurately if the final mixture is to come out right.'

> It should be here noted that most scholars believe Walter Benjamin's last ever act was to ingest a whole phial of morphine pills.

'The clown,' said Porlock, from the deckchair, 'the clown believes he has the ear of children everywhere, even the ear of child Stefan.'

Pause.

'The filthy clown loves radio,' added Porlock.

'Radio,' mused Mr Tal, ' . . . thus I was able to listen to Hitler's Reichstag speech. You can imagine the effect.'

'He got fewer laughs?' inquired the rentman.

Pause.

'This brings me,' said Mr Tal, 'to the end of my twenty minutes. I hope they have not passed too slowly for you.'

'Off. Turn him off,' begged Painter, 'It's what the switches are for.' Mr Tal touched his invisible microphone as if he were steadying air that might otherwise crash. 'The radio listener,' he said, 'welcomes the human voice into his house like a visitor.'

'No, no more human voice,' said Porlock, 'Not here.' He then glanced at me, and whispered 'Turn him off.'

I slowed the swing, coming into land.

'Turn him off,' repeated Porlock.

'Dear Invisible Listeners –' began Mr Tal.

'Off!' cried Porlock.

Porlock rose from his deckchair, his Newtonian throne, and hit Mr Tal hard about the head. Damned words, muttered Porlock. He had walloped Mr Tal with a copy of *Picture Post*, rolled up tight and hard. Like a huge great lucifer. Mr Tal's wiry glasses flew off, and he bent and fumbled to retrieve them. 'Dear Invisible Listeners,' said Mr Tal, again. Painter kicked him deep within the guts, and Mr Tal folded. Bloody words. 'No reader,' gasped Mr Tal, 'has ever closed a just-opened book with the finality' (he winced) 'with which the listener switches off the radio.'

'Exactly,' said Porlock. He tried to kick Mr Tal in the head but missed. 'Pissed,' said Painter.

'Dear Invisible Listeners,' said Mr Tal. He seemed to be forgiving whoever they were that beset him.

Silence.

Herr Tal was, at last, clean off the air. Once more he sat, cross-legged, on the earth.

'Now,' said Porlock, 'for an *in*human voice.' He returned to his deckchair.

'Right-eo,' said the rentman, '– Just a tick.' Taking over from Porlock, the rentman tiptoed through the air of Europe; and, on and on he went until stopped short and sudden by the voice of a sad clarinet.

> 'The headmaster at our school, a primary school, loved classical music, and always had some playing as we walked into assembly. Most days it was, I have since learnt, Mozart's 2nd Movement from the Clarinet Concerto. . . .'

As a solitary curve of sound broke over the dark and the cold, I could see, all about me, the pale people of Little Moscow, a thousand Happy Housewives in the strong arms of a thousand Happy Husbands. Utopia was their ballroom, and each tenant and his wife were moving in perfect step as they mirrored, with arched and slowly whirling bodies, the climbing and descending of the inhuman song of the sad clarinet. Ten thousand ballroom classes shimmered across New Jerusalem.

As I looked on, from the swing, Mr Tal stooped and approached my ear. 'An infant prodigy and *enfant terrible* all in one,' he hissed, 'tells tales from the school of dreams.' But I did not care, for my eye was now drawn to the words that were stenciled and nailed to the back of each Happy Husband. Here I read: 'Fish and Chips – Come to Park Fisheries, 32 Little Oxhey Lane, for all Wet, Dried, and Fresh Fish. Cleanliness, Civility, Courtesy.' I then saw that, high above the ballroom tenants, high in the empty sky, someone had lovingly typed the words 'J.O. Knight – Fruitier, Florist, Greengrocer, 30 Little Oxhey Lane'; and here, too, I read the self-same curse, 'Cleanliness, Civility, Courtesy,' words now sung by all who appeared to dance. 'Cleanliness, Civility, Courtesy . . . Cleanliness, Civility, Courtesy . . . Cleanliness, Civility, Courtesy.' But, just as their terrible song was about to hit the tin roof of Heaven, Painter threw himself at the wireless origin of it all, hoisted high his spade, and crashed it down in intimate assault. And, as he struck, Mozart, bloody Mozart, fell, bit by bit, from the crumbling machine, and then there was peace, peace like you only get around here when it's pissing down, or when you stick your head out of a flaming window desperate to recall the tears of London, the sigh of traffic, and the foot-falling of a hundred men all off, off together.

Silence.

'And what do I hear?' asked Mr Tal, still at my side, my ear.

I said nothing.

'The factory sirens,' he answered himself, and walked away.

'And what do we *not* hear?' said the rentman, 'What do we *not* hear round here?' He spoke, as ever, from the cold settee.

'The sound,' said Porlock, 'of a reply when we cry to London.'

'Listen!' whispered the rentman.

Silence.

*West Herts and Watford Observer*
December 4, 1953

Dear Editor,

I wrote to the British Transport Committee regarding an anomaly which enabled said body to extract double fare from the ignorant public. That was October 26. I then had an acknowledgement under reference G4807/H997 dated October 28, to say that the matter was receiving attention. Since then: nothing. Or, to quote Hamlet, 'the rest is silence.'

Yours, Mr. F.G. Vandenburg
124 Woodhall Lane, South Oxhey.

And there I sat, my hands frozen to the chains of the swing. There were now no dancing couples, nor letters in the sky. It was all like nothing, nothing much. And so I watched as Mr Tal fished from a dripping pocket a sodden handful of foreign stamps, and Johanna, at her Singer, held a tiny white dress up to the light of the moon.

'We might as well,' said Porlock, 'be living on the moon.'

'Like cosmonauts?' asked the rentman.

'Undoubtedly,' said Porlock.

'For many of us, moving to Oxhey from London felt like living on another planet. . . .'

'I wonder,' said the rentman, 'if God ever gets to the moon.'

'I believe he sends his Son,' remarked Porlock.

*Minutes of the St Albans Diocesan Advisory Committee*
March 10, 1977

The Statue of the Risen Christ in All Saints Church, South Oxhey, erected in 1953, is quite unsatisfactory; the figure seems totally unrelated to its setting – the impression is of an astronaut doing a space walk.

Mr Tal put back in his tearful pocket the sodden handful of stamps. He had returned to the tree and its quotations.

'The damp boredom of post-war Europe,' muttered Mr Tal, adding a note to one particular quotation. 'When yawning,' he continued, 'the human being opens like an abyss.' Mr Tal looked around for a response. Nothing. Porlock opened like an abyss. Mr Tal tried again: 'People who are not bored cannot tell stories.' Again nothing. But Mr Tal would not let sweet boredom go. 'We penetrate mystery,' he said, 'only to the degree that we recognize it in the everyday world.' At last, here and now, there was a response, from the settee, the rentman lifting a hand to catch the eye of Mr Tal who looked across, hopeful of, at last, some interest. The rentman, however, only wished to know if Mr Tal had finished yet because he, the rentman, had to lock-up soon.

Mr Tal looked down at his empty hands. 'A few dozen million minutes,' he said, 'make up a life of forty-five years.' The rentman took off his watch, stared at it, held it to his ear and shook it, with all possible force.

'A dozen million,' said Porlock, 'That's two minutes for each one.'

'Each what?' said the rentman.

'I can't remember,' said Porlock.

'For the Jews,' said Mr Tal, 'every second was the straight gate through which –'

'Christ, I'm bored,' said Porlock.

'Ah!' said the rentman, 'and do you think Christ himself was ever bored?'

'Who?' said Johanna.

'Christ,' I said, 'Jesus Christ.'

'Not *him* again,' said Johanna.

'Yes, Him,' said the rentman. 'Do you think He, like us, like us in every other way, was ever bored?'

'I don't know,' said Johanna.

'Well, if he were,' said the rentman, 'do you think, him being a carpenter, he'd knock up any toy ducks or monkeys-on-sticks? I mean, if he, our Lord, really had time on his hands.'

'Were at a loose end,' said Porlock.

'With time to kill,' said the rentman.

'Between jobs.'

'Or crosses.'

'And bored to death.'

'No, it was the nails.'

'Sorry?'

'The nails. That's what killed him, the nails – on his hands.'

'Not time?'

'No, not blooming time – that's what he had to kill.'

There was a pause.

'For the Jews,' said Mr Tal once more, 'every second was the –'

'Thank you, Herr Tal,' said Porlock, as if a compere. Zionist comedian, he thought, get him off before he dies – can't be long. Porlock had slowly stood up.

Slaughtered. Still dodgy on his pins. 'I think,' he said, 'I think we need to move right along, along' (he swayed) '– if we, here, us, all of us, are somehow to raise the uproar with which we can' (he swayed again) '– finally Outwit the Enemy.'

'Right,' said the rentman. Eager, he too rose to his feet. 'So, how do we raise the requisite uproar? Now that Mr. Victor Painter has quite buggered the radiogram?'

'We need . . . ,' said Porlock. He made it clear he was thinking.

'Yes?' said the rentman, drawing closer to the wayward thinker.

'We need,' said Porlock, 'a gramophone player.'

'Brilliant!' cried the rentman. Pause. 'And do we have one?'

'By no means,' said Porlock, waving his cigarette.

'That's a blow, and no mistake,' said the rentman, turning away.

'Or, at least, not yet . . . ,' said Porlock.

*Estate News*

October 1950

The Community Association are pleased to announce that they have received a grant of £18 from the Local Authorities toward the purchase of a gramophone.

Silence; a silence then broken by Porlock. 'Seeing,' he began, 'seeing that as yet' (sway) 'we have no gramophone among us' (sway) 'let us, as an interim, pro-tem measure' (sway) 'avail ourselves of our only other ready source of music' (sway). He gathered himself and concluded: 'I hereby commend, therefore, to the Committee here gathered, that well-known miracle of desuetude – Herr Tal's frozen typewriter!' Porlock flopped back to earth.

'Music?' said the rentman, 'From a typewriter?'

Mr Tal nodded. 'In the typist's manual dexterity,' he said, 'the petty-bourgeois sterility of the piano *étude*.'

'Exactly,' said Porlock, from the frozen earth, 'Play, typist, play!' I looked around to see Johanna exchanging packing case for whist table, and sewing machine for writing machine. There were chilblains on her fingers, but still she began to operate the stiffened metal piano, all the while staring up at the sky.

*Her Majesty's Inspectors' Survey*
*of Further Education*
1954

> The Evening Institute has no less than ten typewriters. The machines are placed on firm tables. In some classes reasonable progress has been made, and good fingering habits are being acquired.

'The sterility,' said Mr Tal, 'of the piano *étude*.'

'Sterility?' said the rentman. That's not what he had heard.

'But, what use a piano,' said Porlock, 'in overcoming those who, nightly, would surround us?' He paused. 'They do,' he said, 'still surround us?' He sought assurance.

'Yes, yes,' said the rentman cheerily, without looking.

Silence. Silence as Johanna abandoned the piano for her original machine, the Singer, and sewed. Tiny white dress.

'So, what'll we do?' said Painter.

'Yes, what shall we do even as we wait?' said Porlock, arising.

'Wait for *what*?' said Painter.

'Wait for the *waiting cars*,' said Porlock, '– wait for them *to leave*, that is.'

'How about *sleep*?' suggested the rentman. 'This being,' said the rentman, 'a *dormitory* estate.' He beamed, proud of the fact.

> 'For years I used to get up at seven in the morning to catch the train into Harrow for the regular twelve-hour shift at Kodak, and so I used not to get back home until nine in the evening. . . .'

'Bedtime has come,' said Mr Tal, busy among his quotations.

'And with it, such as sleep,' said Porlock.

'Or not,' murmured Johanna.

'As the case may be,' said the rentman.

'There being among us,' said Porlock, 'a Fifth Column of Insomniacs.'

'Who are, in number, four times –,' boasted the rentman.

'Yes, four times, they say –,' echoed Porlock, swaying.

'Four times the National Average,' confirmed the rentman, almighty pleased with this exception to the British rule.

> 'In the early days we often went to bed hungry - not the children, of course, but me and my husband. It's hard to sleep when you're hungry.'

'So, do not think,' said Porlock, 'that, out here' (sway) 'in our Utopian beds, we all sleep with sleep.'

'But where there *is* sleep –,' said the rentman.

'Yes?' said Painter.

'There are *dreams*,' whispered the rentman.

'And *does* your child have nightmares?' said Porlock.

Painter didn't know, didn't ask.

Johanna's head was now beginning to tumble and fall over the sewing machine. She was, she said, preparing for a christening, but I could see she was on the very shoulder of sleep and spoke busily to herself.

Mr Tal was now close to her side, close enough to ease poison into her ear.

'Telepathic girl,' he said.

'Monstrous misconception,' she said.

'I'd like to know your thoughts,' he said.

'Men who carry razors,' she said.

'Nocturnal thoughts,' he said.

'Coughing, Eyestrain, Headaches,' she said.

'Nocturnal thoughts of a proletarian woman,' he said.

'Nerves, Stomach Pains, Signs of Unusual Bleeding,' she said.

'I'd like to know your thoughts,' he said.

'A queer nativity,' she said.

Pause.

'Suicides,' observed Mr Tal, 'from disappointed love still occasionally occur.'

*West Herts and Watford Observer*
April 16, 1953

Mr. Robert George Judd, a 34 year-old man from the LCC Oxhey estate, was found drowned on Putney foreshore in London. It is believed that Mr. Judd, a married man, had committed suicide after becoming involved with another woman.

*Builders on the South Oxhey LCC Estate*

**Figure 9.1**

Steam Roller, Oxhey Council Estate, c.1948.
Straight lines, new shadows, shining men.

## SCENE NINE

# STILL THE FROSTED GARDEN AT NIGHT

Mr Tal looked around, turned from Johanna, heaved up his cold trousers and began to limp to and fro across the frosted garden, creating as he walked a green path in the white. He sighed, then spoke. 'The great authentic symbol for the permanence of love,' he said, 'has always been the single night of love before death.'

'Exactly,' said the rentman, cheerily, from the frozen settee.

'Only now,' added Mr Tal, 'it is not the night of love.'

'Exactly,' said the rentman, cheerily.

'It is not the night of love,' continued Mr Tal, 'but the night of *impotence*.' This last word he whispered.

Mr Tal continued to limp to and fro, and the green grew greener.

'Something to eat?' asked the rentman, 'Before the morning?'

'*You*,' said Mr Tal, 'You sleepily reach out to the bread-basket for a madeleine.' The rentman looked surprised. '*You*,' continued Mr Tal, 'break it in two, and do not notice how sad it makes you not to be able to share it.'

'And *why* may I not be able to share it?' inquired the rentman.

'Because,' said Painter, 'you can't share bread with dead buggers.' Painter sat on the ruins of the radiogram.

'Fair point,' said the rentman. 'Must be lonely being dead.'

Pause.

'I have hardly ever been as lonely,' said Mr Tal, still limping.

'See!' said the rentman.

'But out here,' said Porlock, 'loneliness is a gift given to all. Out here.'

'Human multitudes,' sighed Mr Tal, 'hurled into the open country.' Limp, limp.

'Exactly!' said the rentman, '*Hurled* we are, blooming *hurled*!'

'Great cities,' continued Mr Tal, 'enclose those within them in the peace of a fortress.' Limp, limp.

'Sweet London!' whispered the rentman, 'He thinks of sweet London! Dear sweet fortress London!'

Mr Tal nodded and looked up. 'Under the open sky,' he said, 'in a countryside – the tiny, fragile human body.' Limp, limp, stop, turn, collapse on the settee, beside a startled collector of rents, if that's what he really collects. 'Tiny, fragile human body,' echoed Mr Tal.

Johanna, still at her Singer, picked up the tiny white dress and stuffed it in the pocket of her gown.

'And yet,' said Porlock, warming himself with a cigarette, 'And yet, and yet, there is, I shall insist, something to be said for all this, all this. . . .' Not finding the word he was after – it may have been 'Nature' – Porlock waved his cigarette at the woods.

'Hear hear!'cheered the rentman. 'We shall never lack for firewood,' he said. 'And besides,' he nudged his glasses, 'each and every tree draws me ever closer to my Saviour.'

> 'It was, we felt, truly idyllic living so close to the country. On arriving, the air seemed so fresh. This was the countryside, the unknown. . . .'

'No!' I protested, from the swing, my feet, for a moment, higher than my head. All looked surprised that I should speak. 'No, no,' I said again, 'every tree is a Judas, a distraction, a deceiver.'

'See!' said Porlock, 'See how Herr Tal corrupts the youth of Athens.' His deckchair creaked.

'No,' I said, 'I learnt that at church.' I brought the swing to a sudden halt. And shivered.

'A breath of ice,' said Mr Tal, 'is blowing through the Promised Land.'

'It always grows cold,' whispered Johanna, 'just before a –'

'Manifestation?' said the rentman. He was, he said, thinking mostly of poltergeists. Johanna could not tell what she was thinking. Sing, sing.

> 'I remember the winter of 1957. My goodness it was cold, pushing the pram through the snow . . . . We were so short of fuel we'd go looking for pieces of coal from the railway embankment. . . . Sometimes, though, we would burn anything, even chairs and shoes.'

'Bloody air,' said Painter. He disappeared into his coat.

'But that's what we came for,' said the rentman, '– *the air*.'

'Victor has clean forgotten,' said Porlock, still creaking.

Painter coughed the night in two, as if to say yes.

'What is more,' said Porlock, 'Victor is, you know, very busy *dying* these days. All too late for him the cure.' Creak.

The rentman left the settee and laid a hand to my head. 'Yes,' he said, 'sadly Mr Painter's days are numbered.' The rentman then raised his frosted fingers and wiggled them vaguely so as to indicate some terrible kind of figure. 'Mind you,' he said cheerily, 'they have been numbered for some time. Ever since You-Know-What.'

'What?' I said.

The rentman glanced at Porlock. Should he say? Was it not obvious?

'The War,' said Porlock, hastily.

'War?' said Painter, from his ruins.

'Yes, the one, they say, you won,' said Porlock.

> ' . . . My husband had been a prisoner of war and had been made to march from Germany to Russia over the mountains. By the end he weighed just five stone. Soon afterwards he had a nervous breakdown. When he came back he was never the same again. . . .'

'I know a man who was in that war,' I said. 'He's short and sits in church, at the back, on his own. He prays with his eyes screwed up, all tight – like he thinks someone's just about to hit him. My father says he's been converted.'

'Hallelujah,' said the rentman.

'Herr Tal –,' said Porlock, '– he too has seen the light. Died a Jew but buried a Catholic. His change of heart came with death.'

'Really?' said the rentman.

'No,' confessed Porlock, 'I deceive. Not so much change of heart as clerical error.'

> The local Spanish authorities in Port Bou believed that the unknown German scholar who had died in their town was called 'Benjamin Walter,' and he was, therefore, presumed to be Catholic and thus buried in a Catholic cemetery. It was a simple bureaucratic mistake.

Mr Tal nodded. 'Medieval Scholastics,' he said, 'described God's omnipotence by saying He could alter even the past. As we can see, now a bureaucrat is all that is required.'

The rentman thought this a fine joke, and added that Mr Tal might need a sense of humour now that he'd lost the belt to his trousers. Mr Tal rose, and began again to limp to and fro.

Trousers, said Porlock, were of no interest; he should prefer, he said, to talk of posthumous conversion and how strange it must have been for Herr Tal to find himself rotting in a Christian pit.

'Christian in the best sense of the word,' responded Mr Tal. He gripped the top of his trousers.

'Best?' said Johanna.

Mr Tal stiffened. His hand pressed at his temple. 'Violent migraines,' he said, 'remind me how precarious my existence is.'

'As do bombs?' asked Porlock.

'Bombs,' said Painter, 'Bombbombbombs.'

Mr Tal nodded. 'Under the open sky,' he said, 'in a countryside and beneath these clouds in a field of explosions the tiny' (he paused) 'fragile' (he paused) 'human body.'

'But what,' said Porlock, 'what of the human body *above* the clouds? What of him?'

> 'In the war my father was a bomber-pilot, but because he was a Communist he insisted that he never be sent to bomb civilians, and the RAF accepted this condition. One morning, however, he returned from a raid to discover that he'd just been involved in the infamous attack on Dresden.'

Mr Tal looked up at the moon. 'Utopia,' he said, 'is realized only by the type of man who ascends into the stratosphere in order to drop bombs.'

'Exactly,' said Porlock. He wandered from his deckchair, lifted a glass of frozen wine and prepared to whisper in the ear of the nation. 'Listen,' he said, 'Listen to Professor Gale –'

'Don't mind if I do!' said the rentman.

'It being Professor Gale, of course –' continued Porlock.

'Of course,' said the rentman.

'– who said to the trees,' whispered Porlock, 'that (and I quote), "Invariably the beauty of a housing plan is only apparent –"' (he paused) '"– *from an aeroplane.*"'

I was, once again, swinging to and fro, and thought of that film I had seen of the Carnival and of how, at the beginning, the estate had been shot from the sky, and we'd peered down, straight through the air, from a plane.

'Utopia,' said Mr Tal, once again, 'is realized by the man who ascends in order to drop bombs.' He had moved from settee to deckchair.

'*Socialist* utopia?' inquired Porlock.

Mr Tal was unsure, but not Porlock, who said he knew a man, both Socialist and Utopian, a man close by, in fact, who most certainly had dropped bombs. 'In fact,' continued Porlock, 'this Utopian Socialist once whiled away a long winter's night dropping bombs upon – . . . well, whom? Whom did he bomb? Whom? Let us guess at, say, an abandoned husband, a tubercular drawing his bath, and a delicate child finally fallen to its sleep.'

'Christ!' whispered Painter, his eyes shut.

But Porlock had not finished with New Jerusalems. 'Or what,' he said, 'what about a *scientific* utopia? What about *scientific* perfection? I mean, to be precise, *atomic* perfection . . . . What about that, eh? That too can be planned by gentlemen possessed of bombs – even, so they say, by *Jewish* gentlemen.'

'Oppenheimer!' whispered the rentman, 'Oppenheimer!'

Mr Tal closed his eyes.

And now,' said Porlock, 'listen to this.' He swayed, still slaughtered, and waved head-high *The County of London Plan*. 'Right here,' he said, 'right here, in this, the Book of Us, the Book of How We All Came to Be Here, I have read –'

'Yes yes . . . '

'I have read –'

'Yes yes . . . '

'That –'

'Yes . . . '

'"That weapons of *mass* destruction,"' read Porlock, '"from the air may yet –"' (he paused) '"– be *perfected*."' Porlock swayed, muttered the words 'Jewish gentlemen,' and leered at Mr Tal and the deckchair.

'This era,' said Mr Tal, 'is preparing to do away with the inhabitants of this planet.'

'This *area*?' said the rentman, 'I shouldn't think so.'

Mr Tal stared at his case. He gave it then a shake and whispered, 'Science sees in atoms an electron storm.' Mr Tal was now a man accused, and so we moved, each of us, closer and closer to the deckchair. Mr Tal nursed his case. An injured bird. 'In everything,' he said, 'there is something monstrous we have to keep quiet about.'

Then, right then, just as Porlock was all for seizing the bird, the rentman hop-skipped away. He was off, he said, for a laugh. A bit of a laugh.

'A laugh?' said Porlock, 'What have you in mind?'

'In mind?' said the rentman. He thought, right there in the cold, thought until such time as it came to him: 'A pantomime!' he finally said. 'Boys and girls, everywhere, a pantomime!'

'Ashes,' said Johanna. She meant 'Cinders.'

*West Herts and Watford Observer*
December 23, 1949

Christmas came early for the folk of the Oxhey LCC estate whose Community Association organized a trip to London to see Mr. Emile Littler's new show *Little Miss Muffett.* Twelve hundred children and six hundred adults travelled in two electric trains and, once at Euston, were given a police escort all the way to the theatre.

The rentman, jack-be-nimble, jumped on the settee, and waved as if it were Everest, no less. He then, all solemn, switched on the standard lamp. Both bulb and filament winked at me through a crack in the shade, and the mountaineer's gabardine coat shone in the stuttering light. He then turned to me and cried, now a great Impresario, 'Welcome, boys and girls, to *Little Miss Muffet.* Or, to be precise, Mr. Emile Littler's 1949 production thereof –'

'Emile *Hitler*?' said Porlock. He said he was shocked.

'As performed,' continued the rentman, 'by The Little Moscow Dormitory Theatre Collective.'

'Naturally,' said Porlock.

'Otherwise known,' said the rentman, 'as Messrs Porlock, Painter and Yours Truly together fart-arsing around in the garden, and all because (like blooming Hamlet) We Have Bad Dreams!'

'Damn!' said Johanna. The Singer had finally iced over.

'Our production,' resumed the rentman, 'captures the true sporting spirit of post-war Austerity. This it does by stuffing a lavish three-hour West End pantomime into a hat of no more than, say, four desperate minutes. Words, much like bananas, being still rationed, we have waved a fond farewell to yards of essential dialogue, leaving an altogether battered and utterly crippled pickle-of-a-panto. Should you be watching this on live electric television link-up, please do not adjust your sets, or indeed your under-things.'

The rentman jumped off Everest and, arm-in-arm with Porlock, headed back to the house to prepare, they said, for 'Curtain Up.' They were followed by Painter, 'that footsore cuckold,' said Porlock.

I exchanged swing for settee and prayed to God that Johanna might join me. She didn't. Instead, she walked to the far side of the garden; and, as she walked, her dressing gown, of perfect stolen silk, caught on a bush and slid from her shoulders and down her frozen back. I could see that it was marked and scarred. Signs of unusual bleeding. She moved a hand to catch the gown as it fell.

'How,' said Mr Tal, 'we safeguard our nakedness.' He rose from the deckchair and hitched up his trousers. He then sat down again.

I turned now to see Porlock and the rentman fling wide the back door and return. To the world, the stage, and the garden.

'LITTLE MISS MUFFET,' declared Porlock.

'**Act One**,' said the rentman. '**In a forest**,' he added in a huge stage whisper.

PORLOCK: We won't, we won't, we simply won't go home till morning!

RENTMAN: Ah! Alas and alack, we live on practically nothing.

*Pause.*

PORLOCK: No hope, no hope, we have no hope!

RENTMAN: No *soap?*

PORLOCK: I'm sorry, but about that I shall have to think.

RENTMAN: What with? What with?

*Pause. Enter a Spiv-like character played, reluctantly, by Painter in a trilby hat.*

PAINTER: Psst, want to know where you can get some nylons?

RENTMAN: Oh whisper it not in my shell-like ear, for I –

PORLOCK: Yes?

RENTMAN: For I have washed the royal undergarments for years – both the camisoles of countesses and the pants of potentates.

PAINTER: One way to pay the rent.

PORLOCK: Amongst others.

*Exit Painter, slowly and painfully. It appears he is dying. Pause.*

PORLOCK: I say, you remind me of your late father.

RENTMAN: How late?

PORLOCK: You remember, the one that died having his photograph taken.

RENTMAN: Oh no! Not him! Not that one!

PORLOCK: All right, Cock, keep your 'air on!

RENTMAN: I will, I will. Besides, I always wait for –

PORLOCK: A bus that does not come?

RENTMAN: No – the fullness of time.

PORLOCK: Oh no you don't!

*The two trudge off.*

## ACT TWO. IN ANOTHER PART OF THE FOREST

*The two return.*

PORLOCK: Lost, lost! We are two Comrades all lost in a wood.

RENTMAN: And Miss Muffett, she too is lost.

PORLOCK: *(As if Miss Muffett)* Yes, I ran and ran, then fell quite asleep, and when I awoke I found I was altogether covered in leaves.

*Pause*

RENTMAN: Lummy, this place is haunted!

PORLOCK: Yes, and the lower orders are hot in pursuit.

RENTMAN: The lower orders?

PORLOCK: Sorry – the lower parts.

RENTMAN: Crikey! Time for a song to keep up our spirits.

PORLOCK: But I'm deaf, I tell you, deaf in my left ankle.

RENTMAN: So much for compulsory education!

*Enter Painter as a huge spider. He appears behind the rentman.*

MYSELF: It's behind you, behind you!

PORLOCK: What is?

MYSELF: The future!

*Exit Painter as spider before noisily returning, still more improbably, as Cookie.*

RENTMAN: But hark, who is that?

MYSELF: Cookie Cookie! Lookie lookie!

PAINTER: Hullo children everywhere. Well, do you know, the other day, I ran and ran, then quite fell asleep.

PORLOCK: Yes, and once in your sleep, I heard you say:

PAINTER: Oh, Clark Gable, *IF* you're able, kiss me once again!

PORLOCK: And was he? Was he? Was Clark Gable really able?

RENTMAN: Or did they, the buggers, put something in his tea?

*Exeunt omnes to comic music.*

## ACT THREE. NOWHERE, IN PARTICULAR

*Enter Uncle Evil played by Painter (still a-dying). He is followed by the other two.*

PAINTER: Now, now for the poison, just strong enough to kill.

RENTMAN: For it is, you see, not just curiosity that kills.

PORLOCK: That kills the cat?

RENTMAN: Cat? Cat! Why ever a cat?

PORLOCK: But what of *Schroedinger's* cat?

PAINTER: Whom?

RENTMAN: You know, the hypothetical cat that, given the paradoxical laws of quantum physics, as advanced by Mr. E. Schroedinger, is at once not only alive but also and simultaneously quite dead.

PORLOCK: The paradox lies in the clever coupling of quantum and classical domains.

RENTMAN: Exactly!

PORLOCK: I bet that wasn't in the script!

*They laugh unconvincingly. Pause.*

PAINTER: But I don't, on reflection, see why I should be the only one to suffer.

PORLOCK: Particularly since several of the audience are, we think, still alive.

PAINTER: Not that I'm one to gossip.

PORLOCK: About what?

*Painter falls to the ground, a coughing consumptive. No one seems to care. Not a soul.*

## GRAND FINALE OR EPILOGUE

*Porlock moves to centre stage to explain that the pantomime will conclude with a dramatic monologue delivered by the rentman in the character and attire of a female cockney gossip. He adds that her words are 'a verbatim extract from Emile Littler's production – from here on, no more monkeying about with the script. Not a jot nor a tittle. No, not a tittle at all.'*

RENTMAN: *(Rapidly, addressing thin air)* Not that I'm one to gossip, Cookie – I mean Mrs. 'Ardcrust, but I 'eard the new shop was frying this morning, so queue there was and queue I joined. And there, if you please, bold as aluminium, was Mrs. 'Iggs, wearing a brand new fur coat – so-called. "Morning, 'Iggy," I sez. "Bin doin' bit of knocking off?" I sez. "Ow d'you like it," she sez. "Real minx, it is." "Minx," I sez, "minx! – then a good match for that daughter of yours," I sez. "And what do you mean by that Mrs. 'Ippy," she sez, nasty-like – you know 'ow she can *be* – "Oh nothing," I sez, 'aughty, "but the 'ole street knows she's throwing 'erself at this young man that's opened up in fish – we all 'as eyes," I sez. "So 'ave cods," she sez. "Ho!" she goes on, drawin' herself up like a stick of rhubarb, "Ho! it's a pity some folk 'aven't got summink better to do than keep peepin' be'ind their curtains – if you can still *call* 'em curtains."

### THE END, THE END

Now that the end had come, the rentman grabbed Porlock by the forearm to draw him closer, for a word, in confidence, just between the two of them, and the gatepost. The rentman was still, he said, 'deep in character' and so kept looking over his shoulder, first left then right, as if to check that no one in the crowded London street, still busy in his head, was near enough to overhear. The rentman then sailed into how he had just met that queer bloke, Mr Tal.

'Well, he sez, the silly sod, right after the bloody panto, he sez it's just like "The English stage experiment *Hamlet in Tails.*" "Oh no it's not," I sez, "It's just a bloody panto." "The pantomime of existence," sez he, quick as shit. So I sez, "But the question is 'Why should I be the one to suffer?'" So he sez, all knowing-like, "Suffering holds the key to the essence of humanity." "Oh really?" sez I. And he just nods and sez, "The Messianic passes through suffering." So I sez, "But all that pain and that, it's all be'ind you." Then nothin – he sez nothin. So a bit nervous, I sez, "I knows where you can get some nylons." So he sez, comes straight out with it, all bold like, "Every carnival has its catch-phrase." "Yes," I sez, "and every bloody philosopher too – like, fr'instance, 'There is an infinity of soap, but not for us.'" "Kafka," he sez, cheeky sod. Kafka, indeed! Bugger ought to wash his mouf out, wash it out with 'ope. And does he? Does he 'eck! Bloomin carries on, sez crazy stuff like, "The historian is a prophet facing backward." "So, it's behind you," I sez. "What?" he sez. "The future," I sez, all clever. Then, dunno why, he sez, "What do I hear?" Well, o'course, I sez again, "The future," all posh. "Mind you," I sez, all 'dignant-like, "him indoors he goes and dies 'aving his bloody photo taken. Just like that, if you please." "The camera," he sez, "gave the moment a posthumous touch." "You can say that again!" I sez. Any-old-ow, then I sez, a bit saucy, "Oh Clark Gable if you're able –" and, all sudden-like, he gets filthy and starts goin on about "male sexuality," would yer believe it. Well, I've 'eard his sort before – e's no better than he should be. So I sez, "What kind of a girl do yer take me for." And he sez, face like a bloody poached-egg, "Why?" "Why!" I sez, "What kind of a question is that?" And he sez, all 'igh and mighty, "The Socratic inquiry is not the holy question." "So," I sez, "what *is* the holy bloody question?" And he sez, "Why?" And I sez, "Why *what*?" And he just sez, "Why?" So I sez, "Look yer cheeky bugger, now for the poison, just strong enough to kill." "Murder," he sez, all uppity, "murder is suspected." "You ain't been murdered," I sez, "Pull the other one." So he starts changin his tune, shakin his nut, and sez, "Suicide." "Seaside?" I sez, "Long bloody way to the seaside." Tho' there is Margate. "Any 'ow," I sez, "what you got in that case?" So he sez, "Secret Germany." "Ooh," I sez, all knowing like, "you mean like that lot what wanted to blow up bloody Adolf 'Itler?" and he sez nothing. So I sez, "Oh, pardon yer Fuhrer! Must 'ave been thinkin of Claus von Stauffenberg – he 'ad a case wot went bang, he did." Well, he then sez nuffin! Just legs it, down the street, and up the so-called woods, all shiverin-like.'

Pause.

Pause.

I turned to see if Mr Tal, low in the deckchair, would respond. Throughout it all, he had been writing away to himself, head bowed, but now he scrambled to his feet and dashed headlong back into the flickering house, and with him stumbled the rentman who, even as he stumbled, was throwing off all the vain and glorious things he had put on to make him a vain and glorious woman. Porlock wolf-whistled and the rentman blushed. 'Cheeky sod,' said the rentman, adding that the two of them, he and Mr Tal, were 'off to do some bloomin Shakespeare, don't you know.' The dormitory estate held its dormitory breath and Porlock joined me on the stiff settee, his legs stretched out like a pier.

Then, all and sudden, we heard Mr Tal declaiming in the kitchen, his voice swollen by a megaphone, a machine made to torture words. 'Again and again in Shakespeare,' blared Mr Tal, 'battles fill the last Act; and kings, princes, attendants and followers "*Enter, fleeing.*"'

'Fleeing,' echoed Painter.

'The moment,' blared Mr Tal, 'in which they become visible to spectators brings them to a standstill.' The megaphone crackled.

'Standstill,' said Painter.

'Their entry,' blared Mr Tal, 'into the visual field of non-participating persons allows the harassed to draw breath.' The megaphone crackled again.

'Breath,' said Painter.

Mr Tal, his loudhailer now howling, was coming to the end. It would be the last crackle of his Great Shakespearean Interpretation. 'Our reading of this formula,' he blared, 'is imbued with expectation of a place, a light, a footlight glare –.'

'Yes, yes . . . ,' said the rentman.

'– a footlight glare in which,' howled the hailer, 'our flight through life may be likewise sheltered in the presence of on-looking strangers!'

With this, Mr Tal kicked open the back door of the house, and, with the rentman at his side, rushed pell-mell back into the astonished garden. They themselves had, it seemed, '*Entered, fleeing.*' Mr Tal was holding grimly to both his case and trousers, while the rentman was feeling for the pens that stood, ever loyal, in his uppermost pocket. I could see no one pursuing the two men – no army, no Egyptians, no furies, no poets, no bloody great spider; but it was clear, said Porlock, from the panic in their pants that they really had '*Entered, fleeing.*'

Once back in the garden, their flight was arrested. Nailed. They turned and looked towards the settee where we sat, Porlock and I. Whether they saw us I am not sure, but they were certainly looking in our direction. There they stood and they stared. And then it came to me that *we* might just be the onlooking strangers of whom Mr Tal had spoken, and for whom he had so hoped.

I closed my eyes, for a second, but Mr Tal was still there, setting down his case while the rentman re-arranged his pens. And both seemed just about to draw a breath when a huge flash-camera peered out from the window upstairs and, for an instant, quite ruined the dark. Mr Tal was clearly caught, clearly caught in the light and the shock of it all. And there, up there, at the window, was Romeo, slicking back his fine hair. Romeo smiled then spoke: 'He died,' said Romeo, 'having, you see, his likeness taken – at but the flick of a switch.'

*Grocery Van*

**Figure 10.1**
Co-Operative Van, Oxhey Council Estate, c.1948.
As the boys keep watch, another mobile man prepares his getaway van, and the girl she wonders if anyone will ever run off with him.

## SCENE TEN

# THE CORONATION AND THE BEAUTIFUL POURING RAIN

Mr Tal yawned in the kitchen. 'I have not gotten up this early in years,' he whispered. He had burnt the toast, again; the grill had failed him, again. A fearful oven, it was. He peered into the empty bread-tin, shrugged and began to scrape the burnt face of the toast. He then began to spread with margarine the toast that was now as cratered as a blackened moon. The clumsy man cursed. Difficult, this was all so difficult – not least, not least because the formica top of the small kitchen table was covered with the scrambled lungs of an unnamable engine. Painter had been working at the table, and now there was, as Mr Tal could see, no clear space, no flat earth. So where in the universe could he spread his burnt moon? The crisis lay before him. But Mr Tal would not be overcome. He balanced his case on top of the lungs and turned the level surface of the case into a species of table. Ad hoc, it was. A kind of altar. He seemed to think this an excellent solution. The altar wobbled.

'I have,' said Mr Tal, 'a whole house to myself.' I coughed to remind him that I too was there, on the stool, but Mr Tal looked clean through me. 'I started the day,' he said, 'with a bath.'

'Me too,' I said, still hoping he might see me.

By now, the kettle on the oven was beginning to scream. Blue murder, or worse, it screamed. But it was as if Mr Tal was hard of hearing, the way he did not move and just stared through the window at all the rain that fell.

'It is,' he said, 'a beautiful early morning.'

Mr Tal finally lifted up the kettle. It had screamed and sworn its last. He then poured the boiling water in the direction of a huge tin mug, but the kettle knocked the mug, and the mug leapt to the grey linoleum floor. The floor of Zion. At last, Mr Tal seemed to notice me, and pointed to the disaster far beneath him. As he pointed, he spoke, as if it were a virtue, of his 'inability to make a cup of coffee.'

I thought he was about to take a bow, like the waiters I had seen at a holiday camp, great and famous men who were cheered to the ceiling every time they dropped all the plates – the more almighty the disaster, the more almighty the cheer. But Mr Tal didn't take a bow. He sought no applause; instead, he shook a bottle of milk to confirm his suspicion that it was altogether empty. He then got to his feet and limped off to the door at the front of the house.

> 'In the very early days there was a ferocious Milk War between the Co-Op, the Express Dairy, and Braziers. It got so serious that Mr. Brazier would often collect newly-arrived families at the railway-station with a young lady employee called Chelsea; he would then drive the family to the Estate Office to collect keys, drop them off with Chelsea, and finally catch them on the way out to elicit milk orders. Eventually, Mr. Brazier was so successful he split the estate with the Express Dairy man, and the Co-Op roundsman gave up. The Co-Op man had only one arm.'

Mr Tal came back. He grinned and lifted up high a whole new bottle of milk. A valedictory gift from the Co-Operative gods. 'Every morning,' he said, 'brings us news from all over the world.'

He then paused to stare at the newspaper. It lay on the table, somehow, and it whispered to Utopia that today, this very day, and everywhere, was Coronation Day. 'News from all the world,' said Mr Tal again.

'Yes,' I said.

'And yet,' he said, '– and yet, we are poor in remarkable stories. Why is that?'

I said I didn't know.

'It is because,' he said, he put his toast butter-side down on the new queen's face, 'It is because no events reach us without being permeated by explanations.' Mr Tal rescued the toast but could do nothing for the face. 'No events,' he said, 'no events reach us.'

'Exactly!' said someone. It was the rentman, who stood outside, visible through the kitchen window, a window that, on our side, was running with the breath and tears of condensation. The rentman tapped on the glass, tap-tappy-tappy-tap-tap (caesura) tap-tap, then breezed into the kitchen, whistling. He was whistling, he said, for both England and St George. Once inside, the rentman's spectacles steamed up so quickly that he marched straight into the kitchen table and knocked to the floor the lungs of the unnamable engine. Having met, he said, so abruptly with the table, he felt he might as well sit down at the blooming thing. He then pulled a handkerchief from his pocket, wiped his glasses, put them back on again and bent down low to squint at the face of the Queen to-be. It had butter on it, the face. As for the rentman, he had ears, I now saw, that stuck out like indicator signals on the sides of an old-fashioned car. 'Looks like Chelsea,' he said, still squinting.

Pause.

'Last night,' said Mr Tal, 'I dreamed I had company.'

'Company, eh?' said the rentman. His ears indicated. Both ways at once.

'Women taking an interest in me,' continued Mr Tal, in confidence.

'Chelsea?' said the rentman.

'Even commenting favourably upon my appearance,' concluded Mr Tal.

'Chelsea,' said the rentman.

'She exhibits,' confessed Mr Tal, 'the inclination to flirt with me.'

'Another order for Mr. Brazier,' said the rentman, attempting to wipe a tear of butter from the royal cheek.

Outside, to the front, it was raining, the old asphalt sky hurling itself to the new asphalt road. There was nothing there to see. But when I turned and looked out the back, I saw, at the end of the garden, a one-armed man hopping up and down, and rubbing together the only thumb he had with the only forefinger he had.

Mr Tal also looked out the back. 'Through the beautiful, pouring rain,' he said, 'you catch sight of the Jungfrau.' The rentman looked puzzled. No sign of any Jungfrau. He said that all he himself could see was the Co-Operative man, but that, to be frank, he looked far from co-operative.

'Constant rain,' said Mr Tal, as the man in the garden began to shake his fist, 'Constant rain now eases the effect of this landscape's beauty.'

'Beauty?' said the rentman, still puzzled.

Mr Tal did not answer. Instead, he simply said, 'There is a view onto gloom through whatever window we look.'

'Precisely,' said the rentman, pulling-to the curtains at the small kitchen window.

'Nothing can vanish as irretrievably as a morning,' remarked Mr Tal.

'Or a milkman,' said the rentman.

Pause. Mr Tal then bowed his head and began to mutter. Asleep or at prayer, I wasn't sure. I could not tell how his muttering began, but it ended with a sigh and talk of having 'serenely endured Pentecost by reading philosophy while listening to the rain.'

'Rain, eh?' said the rentman.

'Pentecost,' said Mr Tal.

*West Herts and Watford Observer*
June 5, 1953
CORONATION DAY - AND ONLY THE
WEATHER WAS DISLOYAL!

> The Oxhey estate in the morning was deserted. Hundreds had gone back to London to see the procession and, as the rain fell and the wind blew, hundreds more were indoors with the blinds drawn, watching the Television.

'I was struck,' said Mr Tal, 'by how many shutters were closed in broad daylight.'

'Like a blooming funeral,' said the rentman, '– all those blind dawns.'

'Drawn blinds,' I said.

'Or, the Cup Final,' continued the rentman, '– like a funeral or the Cup Final. In fact it *could* be a funeral, come to think of it. For all *we* know.' He looked knowing, and adjusted the arrangement of his glasses. 'Oh yes,' he said, 'I acknowledge that all Utopia *might*, right now, be watching our dear unbuttered Queen –'

'Un*buttoned*?' I said.

'But then again they might –'

'Be fearful and afraid?' I said.

The rentman looked blank.

'Afraid of the authorities?' I said.

He looked still more blank.

'Waiting for tongues of fire?' I said.

'What?' he said, 'Still waiting!'

Silence. Great silence.

I could now begin to hear, from the front room, the carpet-soft voice of a television all tangled up with Painter's barbed-wire cough.

'I experience the feeling,' whispered Mr Tal, 'that in the next room events such as the coronation –'

'Absolutely,' said the rentman.

'– the coronation,' continued Mr Tal, 'of *Charlemagne* –'

'*Elizabeth*,' said the rentman, in a spirit of correction.

'And the coronation,' persisted Mr Tal, 'the coronation *might* have taken place.'

'*Is* taking place,' insisted the rentman, '*Is* taking place. And, kindly remember, Mr. Tal, that today, in England, we crown sweet Elizabeth, not Charlemagne – Father of All Europe, though he may have been.'

Mr Tal shook his head, thumped the table and barked, 'The coronation of *Charlemagne!*'

'Keep your wig on,' said the rentman.

But Mr Tal had not finished. 'I experience,' he said again, 'the feeling that in the next room events such as the coronation of Charlemagne –'

The rentman howled in a desperate attempt, last ditch, final redoubt, to halt the lunatic. But there was *more*, Mr Tal insisted, much more that *might* have taken place in the next room – not just the coronation of Charlemagne but 'the assassination of Henri IV, the signing of the Treatise of Verdun, and the murder of Egmont.'

'Bugger me!' said the rentman, now persuaded of the miraculous next room and its towering lodgers. He was, therefore, popping off, he said, to collect an almighty great pile of rent. He popped off.

Mr Tal stared at the kitchen chair, now abandoned. 'Only in extinction,' he said, 'is the collector comprehended.' Mr Tal got to his feet, took up his heavy case and limped off in slow pursuit of the extinct collector. I followed, a shadow away, and, as we went through the house, Mr Tal turned and muttered, 'You start to play around with rooms.' I attempted a defence of myself, but it tripped, stumbled and finally fell, face first, as we entered the front room, only to find it had just been invaded by a huge iron double bedstead. Laid out on the bed was Painter, now in enormous pajamas buttoned right to the top. He stared at the ceiling as if to accuse it, or himself, of some terrible oversight. And on an upright chair, set hard against the bed, was Porlock. Dr Porlock. He sat smoking away and bent double, over, he said, 'The pools.'

I sat down on the end of the bed. The rentman had taken up a post by the window and leaned against the sill, his perch. The curtains were, naturally, closed, and the room's only light was the light that fumbled its way out of the box in the corner, the television. This stout Bakelite policeman was now a kind of puppet theatre.

'Chiaroscuro,' said Mr Tal, 'reigns in Plato's cave.'

'Someone is to be crowned,' said Porlock. He didn't lift his head from the pools.

'Drowned?' said Painter.

'No – "*found*,"' replied Porlock, 'I said "Someone's to be *found*."'

'Bugger!' said Painter, who seemed to think he grew deaf.

'He cannot but react,' said Mr Tal, 'with something of the embarrassment he feels after a lost world war.'

'Not so,' said Porlock, 'Private Painter here has not lost a world war for some months.'

The old killer, the Demon of Dresden, tugged at his pajama collar and said nothing.

'May have lost his mind,' said Porlock, 'or his way, or his wife, or his daughter, but not a world war. About that he is most particular.'

Porlock continued to smoke: inhale-exhale, drag-puff, drag-puff.

In the corner, the Bakelite puppet show now revealed a largely wooden throne; but no one sat there, not these days. Mr Tal tapped at the screen as if he longed to touch the empty throne. 'The figure of the fleeing king,' he muttered.

'Kicked the bucket. In his bed,' said Painter.

'Queer place to house a bucket,' said the rentman, from his perch.

'But *who*?' I said, '*Who* kicked the bucket?'

'Bloody King,' replied Painter.

'His Majesty,' said Porlock, 'had had enough of this here life.'

'Enough of buckets in his bed, I shouldn't wonder,' observed the rentman.

'Enough,' said Porlock, 'of receiving letters from Watford.'

'His Majesty received letters from Watford?' said the rentman.

'Oh yes,' said Porlock, 'all potentates did. In those halcyon days.' Drag-puff, puff-puff; he gently blew the world from his mouth. 'Mind you, they were mostly letters that opposed the erection –'

'The what?' said the rentman, startled. He slipped, for a moment, from his perch.

'The erection,' said Porlock, 'of this the People's Paradise.' He slid the hand that wasn't smoking under Painter's huge pillow and drew out an envelope that had quite lost its way. Porlock proceeded to read it aloud: '"January the 14th, 1944. From Sergeant Philip E. Lee James of 20 Upton Road, Watford, to the King's Most Excellent Majesty."'

The rentman made as if both to salute and to genuflect.

'"Your Majesty," read Porlock, beginning the letter, "Tuesday last I walked, with permission, through the Blackwells' Oxhey estate."'

'Tuesday last?' said the rentman.

'Tuesday last,' said Porlock.

'1944?' said the rentman.

'1944,' said Porlock.

'Ah!' said the rentman, 'What a Tuesday that was.'

Pause.

'Mind you,' the rentman continued, 'back then every Tuesday was a good Tuesday for them that could while-it-away talking to trees. Me, I spent my Tuesdays bringing

Mr. A. Hitler to his knees.' The rentman explained that he'd seen considerable action in the Catering Corps.

Porlock tapped ash on the bed. Painter did not protest. And resumed the letter. '"The Blackwells' Oxhey estate," he read, "boasts a fairly large wood wherein much peace is to be found. And there I saw –"'

'Yes?' said the rentman. He leaned his back against the window.

'"There I saw –" read Porlock; he paused before revealing that, Tuesday last, Sergeant James, the sole occupant of 20 Upton Road, Watford, had seen 'a *rabbit*.'

'A rabbit?' said the rentman. He leaned forward, keen to clarify.

'Yes,' said Porlock.

'*Just* a rabbit?' said the rentman. He would get to the bottom of Tuesday, if it was the death of him.

Porlock turned the envelope upside down and gave it a terrible shake. 'Just the rabbit,' he confirmed.

'*So*,' began the rentman, eager to précis the letter: '"Dear King. Please don't bugger-up the wood round here. Permit fourteen thousand soot-faced angels to slowly fall down all the cracks and holes in bloody London for I, Sgt James, loyal occupant of 20 Upton Road Watford, had occasion, but Tuesday last, to stroll, as if Sgt Adam in Eden, through the wood, the wood in question (you know, the one with the peace), and I, yes I, Sgt James, saw there a rabbit. Yes, I clocked a rabbit. Think, then, dear King, of the rabbit."'

There was a banging at the window. Bloody milkman. The rentman did not flinch.

'And did he protest?' I asked.

'What, the rabbit?' said Porlock.

'No, his Most Excellent Majesty,' said the rentman.

'Well, if he did,' said Porlock, 'no-one could have listened, seeing that here we are. You and I, all of us.' He puffed a load of smoke.

'Whereas the rabbit?' said the rentman.

'In a better place,' said Porlock.

'Excellent,' said the rentman.

'But there is more,' said Porlock.

'More guilt?' said Painter. He addressed the ceiling.

'More *letter*,' said Porlock, 'More *letter*. For Sgt James of 20 Upton Road also advises his Most Excellent Majesty that to build Cockney Utopia fifteen miles north of Old Mother London would be All Too Much. Upton Road, you see, is of the opinion that "two hours a day on the Bakerloo Line on top of a –"'

'Seat?' said the rentman.

'"On top of a *day's work*,"' said Porlock, 'Two hours a day on top of a day's work would, thinks Our Man in Watford, be "too great a strain" on the forgotten proletariat of London.'

'Whom?' asked the rentman.

'Quite,' said Porlock.

I peered again at the puppet show and there, slap-bang in the middle, was the empty throne. Still nothing else. Mr Tal stared at the scene as if a dog stunned by its own reflection. 'The beggar,' he said, 'catches hold of himself in the figure of the fleeing king.' Mr Tal picked up his case and, for a moment, looked like a king about to flee; he then stared hard again at the television, and said, 'A man does not recognize his own walk on the screen.' Mr Tal put down his case and once more stood peering at the Coronation.

> *The Queen shall in the meantime pass through the body of the Church, into and through the choir and so up the steps to the Theatre; and having passed by her Throne, she shall make her humble adoration, and then, kneeling at the Taldstool set for her before her Chair of Estate on the south side of the Altar, use some short private prayers; and after, sit down in her Chair.*

'An actor,' said Mr Tal, 'must be able to space his gestures.'

'*Her* gestures,' said Porlock. He passed to the south side of Painter's bed.

Mr Tal looked alarmed, and peered still more closely at the Queen, hell-bent on her private prayers. The nocturnal thoughts of a girl. I wondered what they could be. Then Mr Tal, as if to explain why he had just mistaken the young Queen for a man, declared, 'She is three hundred years old.' A moment later he added, 'I love her lop-sided walk.'

'It's the ermine,' said Painter.

'Blooming ermine!' muttered the rentman.

There was more banging at the window.

I watched as the poor old girl made her way, lop-sided, to the throne. A serious man beneath a tongue of flame lifted high above her head a heavy-looking halo; the serious man hesitated, as if thinking of an unnamable sin. He then brought the halo crashing down upon her. Painter flinched, the rentman whistled and Mr Tal joined me at the foot of the bed. He was beginning to write something. Back of a well-used envelope. He then looked at the girl with the halo on her head. 'The coffin in which the girl rests,' he said, 'is not closed.'

'*Is* now!' said Porlock. He leaned across the kingdom and switched off the television, once more a stout Bakelite policeman, strong and silent.

An arm banged at the window. Porlock banged back. Socratic banging. 'Bugger off!' said Painter. Taking advantage of this to-do, the rentman switched back on the Bakelite policemen and the girl's coffin slowly opened once more.

*The Queen kneeling at her faldstool, and the people kneeling in their places, the Archbishop shall begin the hymn 'Veni, Creator Spiritus,' and the choir shall sing it out.*

Mr Tal, writing-still-writing, rose from the bed and edged closer to the screen while, all the while, the choir sang out.

'Come Holy Ghost our souls inspire,' they sang.

'Faldstool?' said Painter, 'What's a bloody faldstool?'

'Enable with perpetual light,' they sang.

'*Toad*stool?' said the rentman.

'The dullness of our blinded sight,' they sang.

'*Turd-s*tool,' said Porlock, 'It's *turd*-stool.'

'Anoint and cheer our soiled face,' they sang.

And, as they sang, Painter fell heavy and headlong into a tubercular sleep. The giant dreamed giant dreams. He dreamed somewhere, they said, high over Dresden, even as Mr Tal, finally ceasing to scribble, leaned towards the television and kissed the lighted screen, kissing goodbye the girl, the soiled face, the kneeling people and all of old Europe. All that unequal light. Mr Tal paused, then once again kissed goodbye the girl on the far side of the screen. 'Glass,' he whispered, 'is the enemy of possession.'

> *In the meantime, the Queen, rising from her devotions, and having been disrobed by the Lord Great Chamberlain, assisted by the Mistress of the Robes, and being uncovered, shall go before the altar, supported and attended as before.*

'As I kissed her,' whispered Mr Tal, 'I noticed that her cheek was made of ivory.' He then pulled open his case and drew out the photograph of a beauty, a staggering beauty, one just like the beauty who had posed so patiently throughout National Corset Week, a woman in part uncovered. "Berlin,' he said. 'Mannequin,' he said. I nodded, though I thought that she was real and that she breathed.

'Her cheek was made of ivory,' said Mr Tal again, but he himself now looked as if made of ivory. I said as much, and he replied, 'The moment he touched me I was transformed into stone.'

'*He* touched you?' said the rentman.

'Apollo,' explained Mr Tal, 'Apollo's touch.'

'Apollo's, you say?' inquired Porlock.

Mr Tal nodded.

'I see,' said Porlock. He lit up once more and returned to the pools.

'So who,' said the rentman, now squinting at Mr Tal, 'who, then, would *you* be?'

'A Daphne,' said Mr Tal, 'a Daphne pursued by reality.' Mr Tal attempted to sit on the edge of the bed, but slid right off it, right off the edge. And, as he fell, there was more banging at the window; it was the milkman to say he was off to 'Get the Police onto bloody Daphne.'

Pause.

*The Princes and Princesses, the Peers and Peeresses shall put on their coronets and caps, and the Kings of Arms their crowns; and the trumpets shall sound and, by a signal given, the great guns at the Tower shall be shot off.*

Mr Tal tugged nervously at a curtain. No milkman. He now pulled the curtains wide open, and beheld the wet and empty road. 'Deserted streets,' he said, 'in which whistles and shots dictate the outcome.' He ducked below the window and crawled back towards the bed to rejoin me at the foot. Comrade Painter was still asleep, but was talking. Dresden.

'Dreaming,' said Mr Tal, 'has a share in history.'

'Even nightmares?' said the rentman, still perched at the window.

'Particularly nightmares,' said Porlock.

'And *does* your child have nightmares?' asked the rentman.

'Only when awake,' replied Porlock.

*Then shall the Archbishop say: 'Hear what comfortable words our Saviour Christ saith unto all that truly turn to him.'*

Porlock stared at his laceless shoes as if wondering where they had come from, these partial shoes. He frowned at this mystery beneath him, then turned to the local paper. He had, until now, been sitting on it. Porlock soon looked up from the paper to pass on the good news that the fine and loyal people of Watford would, this very day, be remembering the Coronation with a full programme of Community Singing and energetic displays of Keep Fit, Unarmed Combat and Formation Cycling. The Cycling, said Porlock, was to be led by a holy man, the Reverend H. W. King.

I could now hear the first sound of people, of children, busy taking to the road outside. It was, said Porlock, beginning to look very much like a display of Unarmed Singing and Formation Prayer. I peered but could not quite see the like of either.

*West Herts and Watford Observer*
June 5, 1953
AND ONLY THE WEATHER WAS DISLOYAL
Coronation Day On The Oxhey Estate

In the morning the estate was deserted but, by the afternoon, the roads were suddenly bright with children in fancy-dress: ferocious pirates, a little girl labelled 'a chop off the old block' and dressed all in wood shavings, and ballet-dancers skipping through the puddles. Physically, everything was against this little-London–in-the-country, but the London spirit triumphed as, all over the estate, children ate and sang and danced in the wind and the rain.

Painter woke, a mountain done with sleep and memory. He made it clear that he wanted to look out the window – to see, he said, 'the buggering rain.' Porlock and the rentman set about hauling Painter up, that he might sit and be a witness. Twice he slipped back towards the crumpled sheets, a grey untidy sea, and twice they restored him to his pillows, a grey untidy land. He was finally salvaged, and stared hard at the wind and the rain, and the children that danced in the wind and the rain.

The rentman greeted this world outside, and whistled merrily when he spotted 'That bugger from the Co-Op,' and waved at him, a happy man. To my surprise, the one-armed man waved back. He too was a happy man and was waving not only at the rentman, but Mr Tal himself, that bloody Daphne what would not pay his bill, but, then, it was, after all, the Coronation, poor bastard, poor penniless bastard. 'Storm of forgiveness,' murmured Mr Tal, 'storm of forgiveness.' Mr Tal seemed to consider himself blessed, and the television continued to bleed.

> *When the Archbishop and the Dean of Westminster, with the Bishops, have communicated in both kinds, the Queen with the Duke of Edinburgh shall advance to the steps of the Altar and, both kneeling down, the Archbishop shall administer the Bread, and the Dean of Westminster the Cup, to them. And in the meantime the choir shall sing.*

'How about The Hokey Cokey?' said the rentman. He addressed the Dean of Westminster.

'Not sufficiently farcical,' replied Porlock. He stubbed out a fag on the back of his hand and howled.

'Quiet!' whispered Painter, 'Our Queen communicates in both kinds.'

'Meaning?' said the rentman.

'Forty-nine levels of meaning,' said Mr Tal.

'Like The Hokey Cokey,' commented the rentman.

'*Meaning*,' declared Porlock, 'that your Lord and Saviour is being both eaten and drunk, his own flesh and blood, on screen right now, before your very eyes.'

Pause.

'It is said,' remarked Mr Tal, as if to help, 'that Charlie Chaplin is planning a Christ-film.'

'It's the other way round,' said Porlock. He turned again to the puppet show in the Abbey, the one in the corner, where the infant Queen was busy communicating two ways at once.

'A mechanical cabinet,' said Mr Tal, staring at the television. 'Biblical figurines,' he added.

'This –,' said the Archbishop, '– This is my body and this is my blood.'

'Biblical figurines,' said Mr Tal, 'the clockwork that drives them ticks audibly.'

'Drink ye all of this,' added the Archbishop.

'Cup of tea?' asked the rentman.

'Do this as often as ye shall drink it,' concluded the Archbishop.

'Sugar?' asked the rentman.

Pause.

Outside, right across New Jerusalem, the spirit of London had run amok. A mad and holy ghost. Round Hoylake Gardens, seventy children were juggling four hundred fairy cakes; up Blairhead Drive, an arthritic piano danced on the asphalt; down our own road, a boy of twelve, called Tony Hogg, was giving a Conjuring Display that went on and on.

'I look,' remarked the Archbishop, 'for the Resurrection of the Dead.'

'And I for my glasses,' said the rentman.

'And,' said the Archbishop, 'the life of the world to come.'

Mr Tal trembled at the thought, the very thought. 'I have fallen,' he whispered, 'into the headquarters of the Magic Jews.'

'Magic *who*?' asked the rentman.

'Magic *Jews*,' said Mr Tal.

'Magic *Tony*,' insisted the rentman, 'Magic *Tony*.'

I peered out to spot this particular Tony. He stood by an old black car that was stiff and upright like a dog that begged. Tony conjured on and, just a few feet away, watching from across the road, was the one-armed milkman hand-in-hand with a most beautiful woman. Like a daughter of God, she was. They stood there, together, for the whole performance, so happy to be yawning in the rain.

'Chelsea,' said the rentman. He was smiling at the most beautiful woman and all that he saw of Utopia. It had come, it had finally come. Time, he thought, to hurl a hundred jellies and tread on many more fairy cakes. The tricks are out, he thought. Magic Tony, he thought, has mesmerized a daughter of God, a buggered piano has gone for a walk, and him from the Co-Op is bloody shining. Hallelujah. He was reborn. He had been a bad man of late. He now would do better; oh, so much better.

*West Herts and Watford Observer*

June 5, 1953

GONE WAS THE OXHEY SPACE BARRIER

On Coronation Day warmth of heart and good impulse destroyed the space barrier to community on the Oxhey estate, the barrier that semi-detached houses had set to people used to being all-of-a-family in the same narrow street.

Comrade Painter coughed and slid, helpless, falling in with disastrous sleep once more. Painter was high above Dresden once more. With a smile, Porlock placed *The*

*Sporting Life* over the giant face of sleep and uncapped a bottle.

> *Then her Majesty . . . shall proceed . . . to the west door of the Church . . . And, as the Queen proceeds from the Chapel, there shall be sung by all assembled the National Anthem.*

Seeing the girl finally go, slow solemn Cinderella, the rentman stood to a kind of attention, wiping away every tear from his eyes. The National Anthem was sung and Painter began to snore. A deep and distant trouble. Porlock, who must have just dropped something or other, fell to his knees to recover whatever it was. He had grown weary of Cinderella, and so too had Mr Tal. 'History,' said Mr Tal, 'can claim no more attention than a child's kaleidoscope.'

'Can't find it,' said Porlock. He had stuck his head right under Painter's bed. A kind of crypt it was, or grave, or place to conceal a lover.

'A kaleidoscope,' continued Mr Tal, still thinking of History, '– a kaleidoscope which, with every turn of the hand' (he stared at his lonely hand) 'dissolves the established order.'

'Nowhere,' said Porlock.

'And the kaleidoscope,' said Mr Tal, 'must be *smashed*!'

The rentman rushed to the television to hurl his body before, he said, the imperilled kaleidoscope.

'The historical materialist –,' said Mr Tal.

'Beg your horsemeat?' said the rentman, now stationed before the television.

'The historical materialist,' said Mr Tal, 'has to brush history *against the grain*.'

The loyal rentman was still on guard, his back to the great west door of Westminster Abbey.

'The historical materialist,' said Mr Tal, 'has to brush history against the grain – *even if he needs a barge-pole to do it.*'

'A barge-pole!' said Porlock. He now re-emerged from under Painter's bedstead, but banged his head. As once before. He was just in time to see Mr Tal take up a carpet sweeper and point its long handle at the assembled peers of the realm. 'The kaleidoscope must be smashed,' said Mr Tal. The screen then stuttered and stammered as if it had the fits.

'Film,' cried Mr Tal, chucking his bargepole to the floor, 'Film has burst this prison-world *asunder*!'

Again the screen stuttered and stammered.

'– *asunder*,' cried Mr Tal, '– *asunder* by the dynamite of the tenth of a second!'

The rentman tried banging the television.

'– so that now,' continued Mr Tal, 'in the midst of its far-flung ruins –'

'Ruins,' said Painter, waking.

'– we,' concluded Mr Tal, 'we calmly go travelling.'

'Excellent,' said the rentman, '– with our barge-poles.'

'Our *what*?' said Painter.

'With our barge-poles,' explained the rentman, 'we shall all go a-travelling.'

'Where?' said Painter.

'Where!' said the rentman, surprised to be asked.

'Yes, where?' said Painter.

The rentman paused. He hadn't considered exactly where we, with Mr Tal, would go a-travelling. Was it Watford? Or beyond? He turned to Mr Tal for help, but the old man just lifted up the handle of the carpet sweeper, as if he were Moses ready with his stick to smite the rock in the desert. But this Moses smote nothing. 'A barge-pole,' he said.

By now, the television had finally fitted to a halt, as if an epileptic at the last. But the rentman could not care, for he was new born and would soon be a-travelling. Meantime, he stared out at that wonder-boy who still, with his wand, stood poking at the weather. The disloyal weather.

## SCENE ELEVEN

# STILL THE CORONATION AND THE BEAUTIFUL POURING RAIN

The rentman was ready to speak. He'd been having, he said, a bit of a think. He turned around to face us. A think about where we could all go a-travelling. 'How about the sea-side?' he concluded. 'Margate Sands, Clacton-on-Sea, Foaming-at-the-Mouth' (he smiled an *ITMA* smile) '– blooming marvellous.'

'Foaming?' said Porlock, 'A heavenly resort. The last.' He tapped at his bottle, Coronation Ale, and grinned. 'Though there is,' he said, 'the ticklish question of how the hell such as us might ever reach the sea.'

'A barge-pole,' said Mr Tal. He waved the carpet sweeper.

'Quite,' said Porlock, from his chair by the bed, 'Sadly, however, we do not, as yet, possess a *barge* to complement the pole.'

'But we do,' said the rentman, 'have a *boat*.' He pulled a local newspaper from the pocket of his gabardine, breathed upon his spectacles and wiped them hard. He then leaned his back against the window and, speaking like a radio, he announced, 'Friday August 20, 1954.' Pause. For a moment, it seemed as if the broadcast were over, as if that was it: Friday August 20, 1954. But, then, very sudden, it started again, as the rentman continued to read, saying: '"Mr. N. Kemp of Maylands Drive on the Oxhey estate recently constructed, in his own front garden, a six-and-a-half ton boat."' The rentman nudged his spectacles. '"It is 27-feet long and has an eight-foot beam,"' he read.

Mr Tal threw the carpet sweeper to the floor and sat once more beside me, on the bed.

'"The boat was first conceived,"' the rentman went on, '"when Mr. Kemp was made a Prisoner of War in June 1940. Mr. Kemp had been captured after the 51st Highland Division"' (the rentman again tackled his glasses) '"were cornered by Nazi forces in northern France and unable to retreat across the Channel."'

> *The End of the 51st Highland Division*
>
> Having arrived in the harbour on June 10, 1940 and finding no one there, the British Navy had withdrawn on the 11th and, after coming under air attack, pulled further out to sea. When the order came to carry out the evacuation it was too late. A combination of fog obscuring the coast, the loss of several boats, and the fact that the Germans occupied the cliffs overlooking the town, made evacuation impossible.

'It was, let us agree, not quite Dunkirk,' said Porlock, 'Not quite Dunkirk, let us agree.' He prodded the bedridden giant, with his bottle.

'Stuck,' mumbled the giant, 'stuck on the –'

'No!' said Porlock, 'not in front of the boy.' But it was all too late.

'– the fucking beach,' concluded the giant, 'the fucking, fucking beach.'

'"Mr. Kemp had, however, a problem,"' continued the newspaper.

'No flotilla,' said Porlock, eyeing his bottle, 'No dear flotilla of week-end yachts and fishing boats. None in the offing, none dancing out of the mid-summer mist.'

'"The problem, you see, was similar to Robinson Crusoe's"' (it was that newspaper again).

'The fucking beach,' mumbled Painter.

'"As our readers will remember,"' persisted the paper, '"Robinson Crusoe laboriously constructed a vessel only to find it was too heavy to get down to the sea."'

'The fucking sea,' mumbled Painter, 'the fucking, fucking sea.'

'"For that, speaking roughly, is what happened on the Oxhey estate,"' continued the rentman, now in sight of the twist, the irony, the stupid bloody end. He tapped quickly at his teeth and then announced that, '"The unfortunate Mr. Kemp" – the *poor* unfortunate Mr. Kemp,' he added – '"was compelled, in the end, to pay £40 just to get his boat to the nearest water-way."'

'And where,' said Porlock, 'is the nearest water-way?'

'The River Chess,' said the rentman. He coughed. 'That's near Rickmansworth.'

'Hell, fucking hell,' mumbled Painter.

'Quite,' said Porlock. He held his bottle to his lips, and drank to the Queen.

'Oh, and Mr. Kemp's boat,' added the rentman, ' . . . it is, as yet, un-named.'

Silence.

'Has he considered "The Ark"?' said Porlock.

'The Dead?' suggested Painter.

'The Irony?' mused Porlock.

'One of the last ships,' said Mr Tal.

'No,' said the rentman, 'I hardly think so.'

'One of the last ships *into which one vanishes*,' said Mr Tal.

'I think not,' said Porlock. 'Besides, it is surely not a *ship* but rather the *sea* into which one vanishes, and towards which one is drawn, seduced, enticed, in the end, in the very end.' Silence. 'Is it not?' He rested his bottle against Painter's pillow.

*West Herts and Watford Observer*
July 6, 1951
OXHEY ESTATE LODGER FOUND DROWNED

> At 3.15 pm on Sunday last, Mr. Michael Joseph McLuskey (age 24) left his lodgings in Sidmouth Close on the LCC Oxhey estate with the landlady's two sons, Jimmy and Edward Walsh. The boys returned at 6pm saying 'Michael has got lost.' They'd taken him to a private lake three miles away in Northwood and there Mr. McLuskey had drowned. His clothes and towel were folded neatly and laid in a pile on the bank.

'Few,' said Porlock, 'very few can resist flowing water.' He bent down and picked up that huge virgin-white book I had seen once before.

'Says so,' continued Porlock, 'in *The Greater London Plan.*' He opened the book and touched a pale photograph of the Thames and of hundreds of smiling people, each standing on one leg and undressing along a slim line of London beach.

'See,' said Porlock, 'few people can pass flowing water.'

'Trouble passing water?' said the rentman, 'Who has trouble passing water?'

'Not Victor,' said Porlock, '– least not in his bed.'

Porlock now abandoned *The Greater London Plan* and picked up his bottle once more.

Outside the rain continued to fall – its habit, its way. 'As ever,' said Porlock, 'it rains upon Bank Holiday. God, you see, has no time for the working-class.'

But *the rain, the rain,* I know because I have read, have looked back and read, it also fell on the proud: in London, on the Queen and all the Queen's Men; in Watford, on the Reverend King and his Formation Cycling Team. And besides, and besides, notwithstanding all this rain, out here I could still hear the cloudless, heavenly blue sound of an ice-cream van, its automated siren-song drawing every other child to its cloudless side. I could see them through the window.

'A final ice cream,' said Mr Tal, as if he read my mind.

> *Estate News*
> August 1950
>
> On July 9, a number of coaches will leave the estate at 8.30 am for Clacton-on-Sea. Last year fourteen coaches were filled. If you have not booked your seat please do so at once. Mr. Piper is doing a grand job in organising this outing.

Mr Tal stared at the van and its gay emblems of holiday. 'Nothing is more epic than the sea,' he whispered. 'Lie on the beach, listen to the surf.' He stood up.

'You'll be off to the sea-side then?' inquired the rentman.

'If the Geneva Institute does not send for me to come to America,' replied Mr Tal.

> Walter Benjamin had hoped his connections with academic friends in neutral Switzerland would provide him with a way out of occupied France. His great hope was to follow to America a host of fellow German-Jewish intellectuals, such as his friend Theodor Adorno.

Without hesitation, Mr Tal dragged off his shoes, socks and jacket, and rolled up the bottoms of his trousers. 'I must be on my way,' he observed.

'The Geneva Institute?' said the rentman.

Mr Tal appeared bewildered, like a man at the seaside. Shoes and socks in one hand, and jacket laid over his arm.

'They sent for you, then?' said the rentman.

The man at the seaside still appeared bewildered.

'You know – the Institute, the Geneva Institute,' said the rentman.

The man on the beach nearly laughed, nearly laughed his head off. No, they had not sent for him. And no, he was not going to make it to America. 'A final ice cream,' he said, once again looking straight out of the window – this time straight at all that weather. But, despite the rain, he squinted and shaded his eyes as if the light, despite the rain, was trampolining, despite the rain, trampolining off some crystal-blue sea.

'If the sun were not dazzling,' said Mr Tal, 'you might be able to pick out Dostoyevsky.'

'Or even Romeo,' said Porlock, talking to a bottle he'd finished forever.

'A final ice cream,' said Mr Tal. He then said something about 'Gambling at the seaside.'

'Grumbling?' said the rentman, 'Mustn't grumble, not at the seaside.'

'Enough!' said Painter. He pressed a pillow to his own huge face. Enough.

Pause.

Mr Tal was, once more, my neighbour at the foot of the bed. He put his shoes and socks back on, and unrolled the ends of his trousers. He then stared right across the road, his gaze fixed on the wooden cross. He shrugged. 'The church,' he said, 'verges, like God Himself, on –'

'The ridiculous?' said the rentman.

'– on the *sea*,' said Mr Tal, 'the church verges, like God Himself, on the *sea*.'

'You mean, like Clacton?' said the rentman. He scratched his behind against the window sill.

'But nowhere is like fair Clacton,' said Porlock. 'Besides, Clacton is a distance.'

'As is,' said the rentman, 'any blooming water-way. Ask Mr. N. Kemp.'

'There's always the Lido,' said Painter. His voice was muffled by the pillow he held fast to his face.

'I don't follow,' said the rentman.

'Ruislip Lido,' said Painter. He had taken the pillow away from his face and had sat himself up. 'Municipal bathing-spot,' he said. 'Good for a drowning,' he said.

Painter then slid back down again and Mr Tal nodded as if to say that drowning really was the point of water. He seemed to know all there ever was to know about water.

> In 1941, a year after Walter Benjamin's death, his son Stefan was deported, by ship, from England to Australia as an 'enemy alien.' It is thought that the treatment to which he was subjected when on the ship, where he was under the authority of German Nazis, severely traumatized him.

Mr Tal rose and moved close to the window, almost nudging the rentman aside. He looked through the rain. Finally easing. 'We can now,' he said, 'see land at last.'

'America?' said the rentman.

Mr Tal stared back. 'Leaving Europe,' he said, 'is a necessity.'

'In which case,' said Porlock, 'you have come to the right place.'

> 'When we first arrived in Oxhey we felt like settlers; that was the word we kept using, "settlers."'

Mr Tal now pressed his face to the window and murmured. 'I am pointing my telescope,' he said, 'through the bloody mist.'

'And what,' said Porlock, 'what do you see? Through the gloaming.'

'Yes, and where is your telescope?' asked the rentman.

'Not to mention your mist,' said Porlock, waving another bottle. 'Not to mention your mist.'

'Not to mention you're *pissed?*" said the rentman. He felt disquiet.

'Such questions,' said Mr Tal, 'absorb salt on their way across the ocean.'

'Please,' said Porlock, 'No More Sea. Let us have No More Sea.' Porlock swayed a little, then smiled. He had made it clear to all Utopians everywhere that there was No More Sea, or at least that for the likes of us and Mr Tal there was no way to the sea, no way back. And just to prove it, once and for all, he told Mr Tal to evacuate his pockets. Mr Tal did as he was ordered.

'And what,' asked Porlock, 'what do you find?'

Mr Tal looked down as if he hoped to find something like sand or seaweed. But all he had rescued was a handful of tiny slips of paper. Twisted.

'Speak!' said Porlock, 'What do you find?'

'London bus tickets,' said Mr Tal.

'Precisely,' said Porlock. 'Forget America, forget Geneva, forget Ruislip Lido.'

'Ruislip Lido!' said the rentman.

Porlock ignored the rentman. He hadn't finished with Mr Tal.

'Remember Mr. Kemp and his waterless ship?' said Porlock.

Mr Tal nodded.

'Remember Mr. Thomas and his fog-draped Pyrenees holiday?'

Mr Tal nodded.

'Remember Mr. Nutt and his unsellable wooden children?'

Mr Tal nodded.

'In that case,' said Porlock, 'you will appreciate that out here we cherish false-starts, dead-ends, and (to speak with terrible candour) *cul-de-sacs.*' Porlock smiled at the stray French phrase. 'Cul-de-sacs,' said Porlock, again. He rose to his feet, hovered over Mr Tal and swayed. 'It is no accident,' he continued, 'that here in Heaven we have been blessed with so many, so very many, cul-de-sacs. They are here for our instruction.' He lurched towards the fireplace and held on, for dear life, to the mantelpiece.

Painter once more heaved himself up and prepared to read another crumbling and familiar book. *Modern Housing Estates*.

'"Cul-de-sacs,"' began Painter, '"can often be used instead of roads. The result is a saving of road-works."' Painter straightened his back.

('The deathbed,' whispered Mr Tal, 'has turned into a throne.')

'"The main two points to consider in the construction of cul-de-sacs are these –"'

('A sequence of images,' whispered Mr Tal, 'is set in motion inside a man as his life comes to an end.')

'"Firstly, that cul-de-sacs should not be constructed so as to create the impression that they are anything but cul-de-sacs."'

('The storyteller,' whispered Mr Tal, 'has borrowed his authority from death.')

'"And, secondly, that at the end of a cul-de-sac may be constructed a footpath to afford a short-cut to a Through Road."'

'Ah!' said Porlock. He had let go of the mantelpiece and was in trouble. 'So, a cul-de-sac,' he swayed, 'is not necessarily a cul-de-sac, or at least not quite? And yet, and yet,' he swayed again, 'if I understand aright (correct me if I err) no cul-de-sac should ever be constructed in such a way as to allow anyone, not even for a moment, to mistake it for anything but a cul-de-sac. Despite the temptation –'

'The overwhelming temptation,' said the rentman.

'– to mistake it,' continued Porlock, 'for, let us say, a Parisian arcade, a tree-lined Gascony avenue, or steep Pyrenean mountain path.' He was swaying badly, very badly, but glared like one who knew all. Mr Tal lit his pipe – the smoke a screen.

Porlock waved thin arms at the smoke, desperate to conjure it away. Defeated, he returned to the cul-de-sac.

'What discomfits me,' he said, 'is that a cul-de-sac must always look like a cul-de-sac, notwithstanding the fact that it may well conceal within itself a secret access, or occult way through to a –'

'Indeed,' said the rentman, 'an occult way through to a Through –'

'Yes,' concluded Porlock, 'through to a Through *Road*!'

'But, the Through Road to *where*?' said the rentman. He panicked.

'Why, to Watford!' said Porlock.

'Say Hallelujah!' said the rentman.

'Hallelujah!' said Porlock. He opened another bottle. For our Queen.

Pause.

'Though there are,' said the rentman, and he grimaced, '– though there are, As Things Stand, no buses to take us there.'

'Take us *where*?' asked Porlock.

'Watford,' said the rentman, at the window, as ever.

'Let us not grieve,' said Porlock. 'It is far too late.'

Pause.

Mr Tal poked his pipe (still lit) into a pocket, leapt to his feet, embraced his faithful case and seized my hand – whether for his benefit or mine, I was not sure. Whatever, as things stood, he was off, off out of here. Cul-de-sacs notwithstanding. He was off. And this time it seemed as if I would be joining Mr Tal, he of the smoking pocket, and he who even now was looking from wall to wall to wall and door to door to door, and saying, 'The suite of rooms prescribes *the fleeing victim's path.*'

'But *does* it?' said Porlock, fussing and swaying, swaying and fussing, 'Can a mere council house, even if constructed in full and loyal compliance with British Standard Speciffiffications . . . ,' (the word knew no end), ' . . . Can such a house, such a loyal loyal house, really and actually dictate one's manner of escape, one's mode of exit, one's final voyage out?'

Mr Tal, still holding my hand, put down his case, and raised his free hand in an attempt to halt Porlock, the runaway man. Mr Tal was eager to respond to Porlock's question, saying '*If*' (this word he stressed), '*If* there really *is* a secret architecture. . . .'

'And *is* there?' asked Porlock.

'Is there what?' asked the rentman.

'A secret architecture?' said Porlock.

'Not a blooming clue,' said the rentman, 'Ask Mr. Tal.'

Mr Tal nodded. He clearly thought that there *was*, on the whole, by and large, and generally speaking. He then picked up his case again, returned to the staircase and placed one foot on the step at the bottom. I mirrored him. 'A half-day's march away,' he said.

'What is?' asked the rentman.

'You must remind yourself,' said Mr Tal, 'what it means to begin the retreat from Paris.'

'No need,' said Painter. He was busy thinking, deep, beneath his bedclothes.

Mr Tal raised his body and his case and myself to the second step; he then nailed his eyes to the naked stair. Still no carpet. Someone, though, had painted the middle part of each and every step. Together we stared down at this illusion of a carpet.

'I dreamed,' said Mr Tal, 'I dreamed I found myself in a labyrinth of staircases.'

'Didn't we *all*? Back then,' said the rentman who had now stolen Painter's copy of *Modern Housing Estates*. The rentman selected a page that was worn, with affection, and he began to read aloud. '"The treads of staircase,"' he read, '"must be not less than seven inches wide."'

'These staircases,' said Mr Tal, 'I have always hated.'

'"With the rises,"' went on the rentman, '"not more than eight inches in height."'

'I am now treading on slippery ground,' said Mr Tal, as we began to climb.

'"And the hand-rail,"' concluded the rentman, '"should not be less than two foot and three inches above the tread."'

With each rise and tread, Mr Tal looked ever more astonished. Then, straight from nowhere, he whispered, 'A sound rises up from down below.'

('Some might say flatulence,' said the rentman.)

'Is it,' asked Mr Tal, 'some falling rock or a person calling from afar?'

'Neither,' said Porlock, 'It is the sound of the Geneva Institute putting down the telephone; or, just maybe, the sound of London not quite caring even to lift the receiver.'

'Bloody council,' said Painter.

'These Londoners,' said Mr Tal, 'have no telephones.'

'And neither,' said Porlock, 'do we hover above a torrent of falling rocks.'

Mr Tal did not appear persuaded. 'The stairs,' he said, 'erupt fragmentarily from the buildings.' He stared down and over the side.

'Piss-artist,' said Painter from way beneath his sheets. 'Piss-artist.'

Mr Tal nodded. 'What is enacted on the staircase,' he said, 'is an advanced school of stage management.'

'Exactly,' said the demon of the stairs.

I lifted my head to see the demon. It was Romeo, and he stood at the head of the stairs. He wore darkened glasses and held a small transistor radio to his ear, although his sharpened body was, I could see, half in love with easeful Johanna. She wore a sky-blue bathing costume and cap, and she clasped at her shoulder the whitest of towels. Romeo's shirt was black and he wore ankle-high boots that gleamed and pointed West; he was tapping his foot to the floor, British Specified (he said), as he felt for America (he said) and its rhythm and its blues (he said). It appeared he had no time for the fool at the foot of the stairs.

Johanna looked at me. She then beckoned to Mr Tal that he might join them. Mr Tal squeezed my hand, took up his case, his body stiffened, and prepared to press on up the stairs ahead. Suddenly, though, he whispered, 'I am unable to climb the stairs.' I urged him on but he could not, or rather would not, go any further. 'I am unable,' he said, 'to climb the stairs.' Then he lifted up high his small companion, that swollen black case, and, with a shocking smile, emptied its stomach, all over the side.

**Figure 12.1** Premier of Rodolfo Usigli's play *The Imposter. A Play for Demagogues*, Mexico City, 1947. The play was also performed on the Oxhey Estate, in 1963.

## SCENE TWELVE

# REMOVAL

*West Herts and Watford* Observer
July 27, 1951
Dear Sir,
I came to Oxhey from Fulham and curse the day we moved here.
Yours sincerely,
Mrs H.H.
(full name withheld)

Today was Sunday, and Heaven had been turned upside down. What furniture there had ever been was gone, and all that remained, in the living room, were three wooden chairs, a straightforward clock on a wall and the Bakelite policeman. Two of the chairs were set towards the window at the front of the house. The window had no curtains. Not now. And on the chairs sat Porlock and Painter. I stood in the very middle of the room.

Porlock was cross-legged, and rolled a thin cigarette, his head bowed. Earnest. Painter sat as if bolted, his back upright and his hands palm down on his thighs. He stared ahead. He was wearing that almighty overcoat again, although beneath the coat a pair of pajamas could now be seen. His shoes were polished but he wore no socks. The knobs of his naked ankles were swollen, and on his lap, wrapped up in greaseproof paper, someone had placed a sandwich. He seemed to think he was waiting for a train.

> 'In the early days the railway station was just a wooden platform and was what they called a "halt-stop"; you had to stretch out your arm if you wanted the train to stop.'

'We're off,' said Porlock, his cigarette complete. He seemed to address the window that the two men faced.

'Turn again,' murmured Painter. He too spoke to the window.

'Off to be found, hand in hand, drowned on Putney foreshore,' said Porlock. He had begun to smoke.

'Turn again,' murmured Painter.

'The Thames,' said Porlock, 'provides all forms of urban escape. *All* forms. Says so here,' he said, pointing at *The Greater London Plan.* It lay on the floor.

'Turn again,' murmured Painter. He had moved to the edge of his chair, and was ready at any moment to rise and hail the Euston train. Am I happy? He disappeared inside his coat. Am I happy? He was checking for a ticket. Am I happy? Or a letter from the Council. What do you think? He abandoned his search and eyed the straightforward clock. I curse the day we moved here. He dragged a handkerchief from a pocket. Curse the day. And gave each of his shoes a quick polish. Curse the day. He then looked to either side to check he had his things. Yes, his things, although he had no companion. But, then, *she*, she had gone, gone home, some time ago.

'Victor is much improved,' said Porlock, still facing the window.

'Improved,' said Painter, to himself.

'And set to go,' said Porlock.

'Go,' said Painter.

'Like a dog in the traps,' said Porlock.

'Traps,' said Painter.

'But why?' I asked, 'Why go?' I spoke to the back of their heads.

'Oh,' said Porlock, without turning, 'the woods, they're encroaching. It's the trees or us. One of us must go.'

Margot Jeffreys
'Londoners in Hertfordshire'

> By the end of 1958, altogether 1,831 tenants had left the estate; that is some 30 per cent of all the tenants who had initially been housed there.

The rentman, who leaned against the wall, shook his head and beckoned me to him. He then tapped at his nose as if at a door, and whispered, '*Rent Arrears*: rent for the house, rent for the wireless, rent for the cooker, rent for the television, rent for –'

'The very zenith?' wondered Porlock.

Pause. Pause.

Across the road, the only bell to hang in my father's church was being rung by an absurd child. Ding-ding. Now quick with terrible passion: ding-ding-ding. Now slow with grey indifference: dong, dong. Like a disaster, it was. Ding.

'Sunday?' said Porlock. Dong.

'Eternal Sunday,' said Mr Tal. Ding. He stood by the door into the hallway, with his case, full once more. Dong.

'No trains,' said Painter. Still looking.

'Only those bound for heaven,' suggested the rentman, born again and again.

'Sleeping cars to eternity,' confirmed Mr Tal.

> 'One Sunday morning I was lying in bed - I was still recovering from TB at the time – and as I lay there I heard a church bell. I somehow got myself up and, for the first time since leaving London, I went to church.'

'Eternity?' said Porlock, 'We have, then, world enough, albeit only just, for a Recitation.' He suddenly rose, turned his chair around and sat down again, now facing into the room.

'Like Stanley Holloway?' said the rentman, 'That bloke off of –'

'Off of *what*?' said Porlock.

'Off of *the radio*?' said the rentman.

'No,' said Porlock, '– off of his *head*. Like me – me all over.' He coughed some blood, and looked pale. But then, in an instant, he was coolly waving his well-made cigarette and saying that he would now 'recount the improbable adventure of –'

'E.J. Trimmer?' said the rentman, still leaning against the wall.

'Why, no!' said Porlock. He was horrified.

'H.G. Maule?' said the rentman.

'God help you, no!' said Porlock. 'My story is of a still more exotic bird of learning.' He sat upright. Eager. Theatrical. Still smoking.

> In 1963 the parents association at Hampden Secondary Modern School, one of two such schools on the estate, put on a performance of *The Imposter*, a three-act play by the Mexican playwright Rodolfo Usigli first published in 1948.

Porlock smoothed his hair and began his Recitation: 'Far, far to the West of us, and at quite another Hour, all things considered, and beyond the reach of any bus, all things considered, there is a Place and Time they call –'

'Watford?' said the rentman. Leaning at the wall.

'No – Mexico,' replied Porlock, his mouth marred by escaping smoke.

('I dreamed,' whispered Mr Tal, 'I dreamed I was exploring in Mexico.')

'And there,' said Porlock, 'out there in Mexico, there lived, as it were, or so to speak –'

'And in a manner of speaking?' said the leaning rentman.

'Exactly,' said Porlock.

'There lived, so to speak, *who*?' asked the rentman. 'Forgive my curiosity.'

'Ah yes,' said Porlock, 'there lived, so to speak, *a man*.'

'Now we make Progress,' said the rentman.

'A man they called the little professor,' said Porlock.

('My Mexican professor . . . ,' whispered Mr Tal, to himself.)

'A man,' continued Porlock, 'who lived in uttermost exile, and was altogether homeless, heedless, and hatless.'

'Hatless?' said the rentman, still leaning.

'I'm sorry,' said Porlock, 'I grow bold.'

'Bald?' said the rentman.

Porlock continued. 'The exiled professor,' he said, 'was, all the long while, teaching the History of –'

'Hope,' murmured Painter, looking down the track.

'On the contrary, Sweet Ape,' said Porlock, '– the History of *Revolution*.'

Sweet Ape checked again the holes inside the pockets of his coat. Porlock went on with his Recitation. 'One fine Mexican day, there arrives,' he said, 'in a motor-car, a stranger, a man from a great university.'

'God,' murmured Painter.

'And he, the well-read motorist,' said Porlock, 'he arrives whispering that the exiled professor is, in fact, the forgotten Cesar Rubio.'

'The forgotten *who*?' said the rentman.

'Rubio Cesar,' said Porlock, '– Rubio Cesar, the Lost Hero of Revolution.'

'I remember Revolution,' said the rentman.

'A Hero,' continued Porlock, 'whom the idiot world presumes is now –'

'A troubled milkman?' suggested the rentman.

'No – *dead*,' said Porlock. 'The idiot world believes that Cesar Rubio had stopped dead, dead in his boots, in the act of threading himself through the eye of a certain mountain-pass.'

Mr Tal decided he should sit on the floor for this. He drew his knees up to his chin and held himself.

'And yet, and yet,' said Porlock, 'his body has never been found.'

('Neither,' thought the rentman, 'has mine.')

'And so, that night, the People,' said Porlock, 'the People, they encroach, pacing through the dark to encircle the professor's fragile house: car-horns, cameras, crucifixes. And all, all those without, they cry to our man within, saying –'

'Pay that milk-bill of yours?' suggested the rentman.

'Why no,' said Porlock, '"Lead us," they cry, "Lead us once more unto Revolution."'

'Not again,' sighed the rentman, who still leaned at the wall. As for me, I moved to stand in the doorway vacated by Mr Tal.

'However, notwithstanding, and in spite,' continued Porlock, '– in spite of the People, our man within, our reluctant hero, he says, he says –'

'Try the bloke next door?' suggested the rentman.

'Nearly,' replied Porlock, 'In point of actual fact our man, he says: "*Just let me stay dead*!"'

The rentman turned his head to Mr Tal and asked him if (a long shot this) he might just know how 'our man' might feel. About being dead.

Mr Tal, on the floor, seemed to consider this. Then, he said, 'The buried man is the transcendental subject of historical consciousness.'

'Quite,' said Porlock, tapping the ash from the end of his cigarette. 'But, between you, me, and the goal-post, little else can be said for being dead. Not even out here.'

Mr Tal nodded, from the floor. 'One is,' he admitted, 'very glad to be alive.'

'Alive enough to die?' asked Porlock.

'Or, perhaps,' said the rentman, 'to lead the occasional revolution?'

'Or,' said Porlock, 'at the very least, the very very least, to –'

'– win the energies,' said Mr Tal, '– the energies of intoxication *for the Revolution.*' 'Intoxication?' said Porlock. He hurled his cigarette at Painter, rose from his chair, his Seat of Recitation, and made towards the door.

'You forget,' said the rentman.

'I do?' said Porlock.

'You forget we have no pubs. Leastwise, none to speak of,' said the rentman.

'None to speak of!' said Porlock, remembering.

'And, besides,' said the rentman, 'for a revolution, I mean a good-and-proper one, we'll be needing more than a piss-up.'

'We will?' said Porlock.

'Oh yes,' said the rentman. He had been around the block of Time. 'What you need is –'

'God?' said Porlock, a shot in the dark. He had begun to circle the seated Mr Tal.

The rentman scratched his elbow. God, once again, had caught him on the wrong foot. 'No,' he said.

'Well, *what* then?' said Porlock. Circling.

'A mob,' announced the rentman. That was what they needed.

'A mob?' said Porlock, 'A mob? Why, then, we are damned.' Out here, they were hard pressed to raise even an intemperate crowd.

'And besides,' said Painter, 'there's nowhere, bloody nowhere –'

'Nowhere *what*?' said Porlock, still circling.

But Painter had nothing to say. He was buggered if he knew *what*.

'Nowhere *to gather*, that's what,' said the rentman, 'Nowhere to gather, murmur, huddle, press, collect, ferment, and riot; no cafes, parks, beer-halls, embankments, public squares, piazzas, let alone –' (he paused) '– let alone a blooming Winter Garden.'

'Winter*Palace*,' said Porlock, 'you mean Winter*Palace*. Winter Gardens adorn our heroic sea-side resorts. The tea-dance, out of season, hopping gaily on one leg. Is there any other way?'

The rentman heard nothing of this, what with his head stuffed full of all the places out here that folks didn't have in which to collect and ferment. 'Trafalgar Square!' he cried, 'We have no blooming Trafalgar Square!'

> ' . . . We used to call the Post Office, the big one down by the station, near the precinct, our Piccadilly Circus. It had no Eros, mind you.'

Porlock nodded. It was all so true, so sadly true. 'Here in Heaven,' he said, 'we have not even the pavements on which to keep un-muddied the revolutionary soles of our shoes.'

'Though there is,' said the rentman, 'the railway station.'

('Someone,' whispered Painter, 'someone please put me on a train.')

'Yes,' said Porlock, as if now seeing a light, '– the railway station! Yes, *there*, upon the platform and the stairs, *there* we may yet become a fearsome mob, a beautiful fearsome mob.' He brushed his shoulder. 'Just ask the frighted child, the frighted, poor-damned-frighted child.'

*Estate News*
June 1952

Representations have been made to secure a further set of stairs to the railway station in order to avoid the possibility of children being crushed by workers.

'Child?' said Painter, still looking ahead. 'Child?'

'Yes, what,' asked the rentman, '– what could the frightful child ever know?'

'*Frighted*,' said Porlock, eager for correction.

Pause. Pause.

'What is truly revolutionary,' said Mr Tal, 'is the secret signal of what is to come that speaks from the gesture of the child.'

Porlock and the rentman suddenly turned, and, for once, they seemed to see me.

'No,' I said. 'Don't look at *me*,' I said. 'Try that flaming Derek Henderson,' I said.

'But he's dead,' observed the rentman.

'Yes,' I said.

Pause.

Mr Tal looked up. 'A messianic face,' (he grinned) '– a messianic face' (he grinned again) 'must be restored to revolutionary politics.'

'Meaning?' asked the rentman, licking the point of his pencil. Ready to take note.

'His Stinking Highness,' said Porlock, '– that's his meaning. As forever, Mr. Tal's meaning will be Himself. He dreams he's Cesar Rubio, some not-really-dead-man, some Secret Jesus.'

The rentman made a note in his ledger. Leaning, still leaning.

'But enough,' said Porlock, 'of Jesus. On with the story of Professor Rubio. . . .'

> It is not clear why such a demanding and political play as *The Imposter* was staged on the estate, or how it was received. It was, though, a hugely popular play when first published, in 1948.

'A story,' continued Porlock, 'which takes still another turn with the arrival of –'

'Maurice Carpenter?' wondered the rentman.

'Goodness me, no!' said Porlock, tapping his knee. 'It is, in fact, the cold coming of yet another stranger.'

'Should form a queue, they should . . . ,' said the rentman.

'And this stranger-the-second –,' persisted Porlock, beginning again to circle.

' . . . a nice orderly queue,' said the rentman. He thought of horsemeat, still rationed.

'He says,' continued Porlock, 'he says, this stranger, that our Professor Short-Arse of No-Fixed Abode is *not* Cesar Rubio, the thought-to-be-dead man, no, not him at all, but merely a man who *pretends* to be the thought-to-be-dead-man.'

'Good heavens!' said the rentman, tapping music from his teeth.

'In sum,' whispered Porlock, 'Short-Arse is in the Shit-House. He being nothing but a charlatan.' Dr Porlock beamed.

'Good heavens!' said the rentman, still playing his slapstick teeth.

'Good heavens, indeed,' said Porlock, 'And this stranger, he adds, post-script, after-the-event, show-all-over, parting-shot, over-his-shoulder –'

'Adds what?' asked the rentman.

'What?' said Porlock.

'What does he add?' said the rentman. 'The stranger, what twist does he add to the ever-deepening knife?'

'Oh I see!' said Porlock, 'Why, he adds that the real Cesar Rubio really had kicked the filthy habit of breathing.'

The rentman played a little more at the slapstick piano.

'It seems,' said Porlock, 'that Professor Short-Arse had somehow purloined the dead man's name and number.'

The rentman abandoned the piano in his mouth, and again turned to Mr Tal, accusing all the while and making furious notes in his ledger.

Mr Tal stiffened. 'We *feel*,' he said, 'We *feel* the sensations of others.'

'Even the sensations of *dead men*?' inquired the rentman.

Mr Tal nodded.

'Not here we don't,' said Porlock. 'Our dead *have* no sensations.' He stopped mid-circle. 'Let us face it, Herr Tal, my philosopher-in-the-shit: you dissimulate. In short, in brief, and in sum, you wear a –'

'Surgical support?' said the rentman.

'Mask,' said Porlock, 'bloody *death*-mask.'

'The mask,' said Mr Tal, 'the mask of non-involvement.' He straightened his tie.

'I care not,' said Porlock, 'whatever you call it – just kindly remove the sweet, decomposing thing.' Porlock felt the lure of melodrama: 'In the name of Jehovah and all His Witnesses,' he cried, 'Unmask yourself, you fiend.'

Mr Tal shook his head, and murmured something about 'Unmasking *others*.'

'Like *whom*?' said Porlock.

Mr Tal was dumbstruck.

'Forgotten your line?' said Porlock.

'Only a bad actor would forget a word,' said Mr Tal.

'But you, Herr Tal, are a pitiful actor,' said Porlock, 'What with all your stumbling attitudes.'

'An actor,' said Mr Tal, 'must space his gestures.' Then, as if he were remembering some fragment of off-stage existence, some piece that did not fit with much, or anything, he looked around and seized his ancient, yesterday-head. After a moment or two, he got to his feet, stood to attention, picked up his fading case and began, very slowly, to limp through the room. He then stopped at an invisible line. He could go no further. 'One lacks the courage,' he whispered, 'to cross the threshold of the hotel.'

## SCENE THIRTEEN

# THE THRESHOLD OF THE HOTEL

Mr Tal had somewhere found the courage of the world. And began to move again. A number of steps. Then, as if performing a mime, he opened an invisible door. He put down his case and sat on the third of the upright chairs. The chair stood by itself.

> According to the available documentation, Walter Benjamin arrived at Port Bou during the afternoon of September 25. After his failure to get the official stamp needed for entering Spain he, and the four women with whom he had travelled, were allowed to spend one night in a local hotel under the observation of three policemen. Only Benjamin received a room for himself, presumably because he was the only adult male in the group.

'And so,' said Mr Tal, 'alone in my room.' He looked down and his chin fell, as so often, into his raised right hand. 'A room,' he said, 'that does not interfere with thinking.'

'Only dying,' said Porlock.

> One of the women who had been arrested along with Benjamin recalled visiting him in his room and finding him in 'a desolate state of mind'; she said he was lying half-naked in bed and that he had a beautiful grandfather watch on a little board near him which he kept looking at.

'A situation,' Mr Tal said to himself, 'with no escape, where no one knows me, my life must come to its end.' He looked around like a man who had considered suicide in better places.

'The air,' said Mr Tal, 'is hardly fit to breathe but one is being strangled anyway.' He took off the belt from around his trousers, escaped from his weary jacket, set loose his tie and tugged at his collar. He was wearing a vest that was stained with sweat, but his skin, a glistening pink, still cut a hole in the grey cloth of the morning.

> At some point late on September 25, it is believed that Benjamin took a strong dose of poison from a phial; his death, it is sometimes said, was witnessed by the four women.

Mr Tal opened his case and pulled from it a small, dark bottle and a glass. He then mimed the action of picking up a watch, the kind one might hold in one's hand. For a moment, he stared at his palm before performing the act of putting the watch down again. He then lifted an imperceptible jug and poured water that could not be seen into a glass that could. 'This glass,' it said, 'has been stolen,' it said. Mr Tal unscrewed the top of the small, dark bottle and acted as if he was pouring into his left hand some pills or tablets that only he could see. He lifted both the actual glass and the imaginary tablets to his lips and prepared to swallow. His hand shook. Then he paused and, like someone who, all of a sudden, thought less of death, he set everything down once more. 'As if dying,' he said, 'partook of the nature of God.'

The imposter, I thought to myself, the imposter. I still stood in the doorway.

'Herr Tal –,' said Porlock. He was, as before, sat facing the road, looking the other way, out to the weather.

Mr Tal looked up.

'– Who *are* you?' said Porlock, still looking out.

'Who was Kafka?' responded Mr Tal.

'No,' said Porlock, over his shoulder, 'Who the hell are *you*?'

'The person,' said Mr Tal, 'who is able to extract the comic aspects from Jewish theology.' Mr Tal fell from his chair.

'Comic?' said the rentman, 'Comic?' He now took a lively interest in the unfolding suicide.

Mr Tal nodded, re-mounted the chair and said, 'I am unclear therefore I am Jewish,' and again fell off the chair. He then sprang to his feet, clutched at his trousers and looked around his hotel room. 'It would be a good idea,' he whispered, 'if people did not notice I was a Jew.'

'Jehovah's the word,' said the rentman. He tapped his nose. 'Best not make an appalling situation still more appalling.'

Mr Tal nodded. 'I am not far from tears,' he said.

'Nor am I,' observed Porlock. He was now standing in front of the stubborn Bakelite policeman, desperate to conjure up a picture. At the same time, Painter struck the naked floor with the soles of his well-polished shoes. Painter seemed to believe that the train for Euston would, at any moment, be stopping outside his house. If it *was* still his house. If he *was* still the Tenant.

Mr Tal looked around once more. 'In Moscow,' he said, 'I lived in a hotel in which almost all the doors were left ajar.'

'Not yet,' said Painter. He peered down the Bakerloo Line.

'In these rooms,' continued Mr Tal, 'lived members of a sect who had sworn never to occupy closed rooms.'

'Not yet,' said Porlock. He thumped the policemen.

Mr Tal glanced at his imagined watch and rose to his feet. He turned an invisible key and pushed at a door of air. He then sat down again and stared at this door. It stood ajar.

'The most beautiful thing,' he said, still watching the door, 'is the view to the sea.'

He stood once more, this time at an invisible window that overlooked steep cliffs and an ocean at night under the fullest of moons. 'I can hear the sea,' said Mr Tal to himself, 'I can hear the dark music of the surf.'

He then stopped. Alarmed. 'The room,' he said, 'the room winks at us.'

'Correct!' said the rentman who had switched first on and then off the light bulb that hung from the ceiling. Bare, it was. No shade. 'Just checking the circuitry,' said the rentman. He waved a huge wooden clipboard. Mr Tal stared at the bulb.

'Hey Presto!' said Porlock. Magic had finally fallen on the policeman and Porlock had his picture. It was an ancient film, a momentous and sad film that, from the doorway, I could hear but not see. The music from the film swept the whole room.

'No fucking train,' said Painter, 'still no fucking train.'

'Hark the sentimental beast,' said Porlock.

The music swept on, wept on.

'I can hear the sea,' said Mr Tal, 'I can hear the dark music of the surf.'

He then, for some reason, turned around and saw, at the window, the real window, the face of Romeo, shaded and as if far away. Romeo pointed a razor finger at Mr Tal. For a moment, Mr Tal stiffened. 'Hitler,' he said. 'Charlie Chaplin,' he added. The face went away and Mr Tal's body was now softened by the music.

And there, right there, as if thinking that now no one could possibly see him or save him, Mr Tal began the slowest of solitary dances. With one hand he held up his trousers and, with the other, his right, he clasped one end of his unbuttoned shirt front. With his right arm now extended, he was like a bird that had lost a wing, and grown, overnight, absurd. The music pressed on and Mr Tal began to raise and then lower his head, for a moment crushing tight-shut his eyes, before suddenly stopping, as if in front of a mirror. Appalled. 'An elegiac beauty unable to dance,' he said, 'unable to dance because –,' he paused and looked down, '– because he had a hole in his trousers.'

The music stopped. 'The film ends,' said Mr Tal. And there was silence, save for the thoughts of the straightforward clock. In contrast, Mr Tal's handheld watch had nothing to say. Mr Tal sat down and took from his jacket, which lay on the floor, what he imagined to be a pen and a postcard. He bent forward a little and moved his hand through the dead hotel air just above his lap, like one who was writing. 'The wheezing of my breath,' he said, 'is drowning out the sounds of my pen.'

> The hotel owner, Senor Suner, remembered Wallter Benjamin's 'painful breathing' which could be clearly heard, he claimed, from outside Benjamin's room.

The rentman looked up. He was kneeling down at the only electrical socket in the room as if checking that too for circuitry. He seemed only to have just noticed that Mr Tal appeared so very sad.

'Glum?' he said.

'Flatulence,' said Mr Tal, 'more flatulence than melancholy.' He spoke like an actor suddenly peering through the footlights and delivering an aside. The rentman winced. Bloody comedian.

There was now another face at the window. This time it was Johanna, trying, I thought, to mouth a message. Mr Tal had seen her too and, fearing she might go, he offered her his chair. Chivalry it was, or was like. 'Telepathic girl,' he said, but the girl did not respond and was gone.

Mr Tal stared at his watch, his beautiful invisible watch. He stared at every second. As soon as a minute had inched by, he picked up his case and peered, squinting, inside.

> Benjamin's possessions at the time of his death were described by the court as follows: 'a leather brief-case like business men use, a man's watch, a pipe, six photographs, an x-ray picture, glasses, various letters, magazines, and a few other papers whose content is unknown.' Scholars believe it is possible that these papers constituted an unpublished work that has never yet been found.

'What weighs most on my mind,' said Mr Tal, 'is the fate of my manuscript.' He closed his case and held it tight to his stomach. Then, in the very next moment, Mr Tal threw his case to the floor, clenched his fist and banged violently at the air. It was the anger of a man alone in a hotel who must suffer forever the sound of neighbouring lovers. Two who should never have come together. 'The *people*,' he cursed, 'the *people* at the hotel.' He slumped to his chair and said, 'I put my hands over my ears.' But it was his eyes that he closed, as if eager to pray. He then opened an eye. 'The praying man,' he whispered, 'is more silent than God.' It was now that he put his hands to his ears.

There was a long silence. Then, Mr Tal began once more his dumb show. As before, he picked up the small, dark bottle and poured out a hand of pills. Morphine, sweet morphine.

'Now for the poison, just enough to kill,' said Porlock. 'Emile Hitler,' he said, by way of reference, or citation.

'Little Miss Muffett,' he added. Again, he spoke over his shoulder.

Mr Tal cupped the pills in his right hand. With his other, hand-sinister, he picked up the glass of water and prepared, as before, to swallow. 'All decisive blows,' he said, 'are struck left-handed.' I looked on and wondered if he would really do it this time, really kill himself. But, no, he dropped it all, everything, both the seen and the unseen, glass and morphine. 'Mr. Clumsy,' he whispered.

'Whoops,' said the rentman.

'Mr. Clumsy the hunchback,' whispered Mr Tal.

The rentman was quick to join in the mime, acting as if he were helping to dry Mr Tal and to pick up thirty-one invisible pills from all over the floor. He dusted each one, very gently blowing each time. He then popped them all back into the small, dark bottle. 'There!' he said, 'Right as is the rain.' Mr Tal nodded. He had received help, although not from myself. This was kindness, the kindness of a fool. And I was no longer a fool, and so simply watched as, suddenly and quite without warning, Mr Tal emptied the bottle, all thiry-one pills, into his widened mouth. He then swallowed and swallowed. Hard, hard. He looked at me and sat down again, this time as if he were preparing to die. 'If there is pain now,' he said, 'there is no God.' He swallowed again.

'Just the National Health,' said the rentman, not looking up.

Mr Tal did not respond. He was waiting for the pain, and it seemed to come, for he clutched at his chest and screwed up his face as if it were newspaper. I didn't know what to do or to say, but Mr Tal seemed to sense this and wanted to help me. 'If a person close to us is dying,' he said, 'we greet him.'

'Greetings,' I said, 'Greetings from Mr. Clumsy.' It was all I could think of.

'Oedipus,' he said, 'has learned to speak.'

I said my name wasn't Oedipus, by no means, and, moreover, that I should not want him, Mr Tal, to die, not at all. Not even if he were but a passing actor. Mr Tal stared back at me, as if he were still lodged in that hotel of his. 'Warmth is ebbing,' he whispered, 'We perish by bleeding.'

> The local, Port Bou doctor who had visited Walter Benjamin on the evening of his death subsequently declared that the unknown German professor had died of a cerebral hemorrhage.

For a second time, Romeo appeared. At the window. He did not smile, he just tapped the side of his forehead. Mr Tal seemed to see Romeo, but then looked down and closed his eyes. 'Warmth is ebbing,' he whispered, 'We perish by bleeding.'

'Lovely words,' said the rentman, pencil tapping at his clipboard, 'Lovely words.'

Mr Tal opened his eyes. 'The public,' he said, 'has an ear only for what the author would have time to utter with his last breath.'

'Last *screaming* breath,' said Painter, to himself, on the platform.

Mr Tal put his shoes back on, made good the buttons of his shirt, tucked its tails into his trousers, now tight-belted, then restored his tie and heaved back on his jacket. He seemed to think that he should dress properly to die. He got to his feet, picked up his case, checked his handheld watch and then waited, as if for a Berlin tram. A moment later, the case dropped to the floor, and he clutched at his chest and doubled up on the chair. His body shook, trembled and convulsed as if he knew the most terrible pain. And then he moved no more. Not at all. Filthy Jew, killable stranger.

> The Port Bou 'register of deaths' records that Walter Benjamin died at 10 pm on September 26. The hotel owner found Benjamin lying on his bed; it is said that the dead man was fully clothed.

I felt for Mr Tal but, before my hand could reach him, Johanna had appeared from somewhere. Perhaps another room in the hotel. Or a night, suggested Porlock, spent running from the evening. How should *I* know? Johanna looked upon the face of Mr Tal, and stooped to kiss his cheek, or the shadow of his cheek. 'Romeo's last sigh,' she said. She then opened the black leather case, such as businessmen use, and tipped its sorry brains all over the floor. Sand, seaweed, shells, pebbles and papers all fell to the coast of Utopia. The girl bent down and searched the coast. The beachcomber then stole from the room.

The rentman drew out his handkerchief and busily cleaned his glasses. Across the road the church bell rang. Backwards. It was that child again. I now heard the back door of the house slam-to, and a few moments later I could see Johanna vanish down the road and, as she vanished, she stuffed in the mouth of each identical door a different piece of paper. Each one, I dream, was the handiwork of Mr Clumsy: one a handbill regarding the end of the world, another a plan for changing the world, another a letter indicating that regrettably it would not be possible to return to the world, and still another a suicide note post-marked the foreshore of the world. And, finally, there was a letter regarding rent, a letter to remind each new tenant and his wife that here in Paradise there was no private property. Out here, no house nor room nor case would ever be owned. Hallelujah.

> Walter Benjamin's grave in the Catholic cemetery at Port Bou was a rented grave. The rental to be paid

for the grave came out of the money that was found upon his person when he died.

Pause. Several minutes marched by, each one checked by the straightforward clock. Then, out of the very blue, Mr Tal opened an eye, just one, and winked at me.

'You think,' whispered Mr Tal, 'this must be the end.'

'Indeed,' said Porlock, over his shoulder. He looked for a cigarette in his pockets.

'You think,' whispered Mr Tal, 'this must be the end.'

Mr Tal seemed now to hesitate, but then he jumped to his feet and straightened both his tie and his face. He could move again.

Benjamin's Catholic grave had only been rented for five years; there had not been enough money found on his person for any longer. By December 1945 the original five-year rental had expired and Benjamin's remains were disinterred.

'One is,' said Mr Tal, 'very glad to be alive.' Porlock smiled. He had found a cigarette. 'Alive,' said Mr Tal, 'in spite of everything.'

It is not known for certain where Benjamin's remains were moved to. There is a memorial to him in the Port Bou cemetery but it marks a body that is no longer there.

'Resurrected, I shouldn't wonder,' said the rentman.

Mr Tal, a modest man, looked down at his shoes. 'I have,' he admitted, 'to make do with what is resurrected only today.'

'Meaning?' asked the rentman.

'Meaning,' said Porlock, 'that it is only *as if* he were resurrected.'

'*As if*,' said Mr Tal, 'is the universal meaning we proclaim.'

'Pity, no-one told the girl,' said Porlock. Smoke crept over his shoulder.

Mr Tal looked puzzled.

'She was of the opinion,' said Porlock, 'that there was no *as if* to your dying fall.'

Romeo was now, once again, at the window, grinning and tapping his temple. 'Romeo's last sigh,' he mouthed, and Mr Tal, still thinking of Johanna, seemed, at last, to understand. 'That we may have missed each other,' said Mr Tal, '– that we may have missed each other as a result of a misunderstanding' (he paused) 'would drive me mad.'

'Just like the girl,' said the rentman. 'She's legged it, you know, to London. Gone there, they said, to sink.'

'One of them,' murmured Mr Tal, 'ends it all in the Thames.'

'Precisely,' said Porlock, rising and turning around, 'and you, my demon, are to blame, you dear bastard, you dear killer, you dear –'

'Murderer,' whispered Mr Tal, '– murderer of the woman who has committed suicide.'

'Poetry!' said Porlock, approvingly, 'Purest poetry!' He inhaled.

Pause.

'Her decision to die –,' began Mr Tal.

'Yes?' said the rentman.

'Her decision to die,' said Mr Tal, 'remains a secret.'

'And *yours*?' asked the rentman.

'Remains a secret,' said Mr Tal, 'until the end.'

'And when is that?' asked Porlock. 'When is the end? I mean out here, what with all these gardens and sky.' He pointed outside. 'There is no end to Heaven, is there?'

'Negative replies,' announced Mr Tal, 'are left to time.'

'In which case,' said Porlock, 'let us hang time.'

'From the nearest lamp-post!' cried the rentman.

'Should we have one,' said Porlock.

Porlock threw his cigarette to the floor, extinguished its life with the sole of his shoe and stared at his fingernails, examining the lines of dirt.

'But if we don't *wait*,' said the rentman, 'what else is there to do?'

'Nothing,' replied Mr Tal, 'nothing but to direct the gaze on the extraordinary event in which salvation now lies.'

'Salvation, eh?' said the rentman. He began to measure a wall.

'Please – my train!' begged Painter.

'*But*,' said Mr Tal, 'this state of attention could –,' his voice dropped again to a whisper, '– could really call forth a *miracle*.'

'Miracle, eh?' said the rentman, now measuring another wall.

'Please – my train!' It was Painter, a beggar again.

Mr Tal paused. He had only just spotted the man at the station, alone on the wooden platform. Mr Tal sat himself down on the chair next to Painter, as vacated by Porlock.

'I lose the best part of my pleasure,' said Mr Tal, 'if I cannot wait a long time for my train.'

Painter blasphemed.

'Marx says,' added Mr Tal, 'that revolutions are the *locomotives* of history.'

Painter blasphemed again.

'But perhaps,' continued Mr Tal, 'perhaps it is quite otherwise.' He took a sandwich from Painter's lap.

'Heaven,' said Painter, 'Heaven help me.'

'Perhaps revolutions,' concluded Mr Tal, he chewed the stolen sandwich, '– Perhaps revolutions are an attempt by the passengers on the train to activate the emergency brake.'

Pause.

> On October 8, 1952, at Harrow and Wealdstone station, in the country's worst peacetime rail crash, one hundred and twelve people were killed and more than two hundred injured, including several from the Oxhey estate. The accident happened at eight-twenty in the morning as a London-bound express from Perth ploughed into the back of the seven thirty-one, Tring-to-Euston commuter train, as it was about to leave Harrow and Wealdstone. This train had, around twenty minutes earlier, collected a number of passengers from the Oxhey estate.

All of a sudden, Painter stood up. At last his train was coming. His peacetime train. 'That'll be us,' he said. He looked down the track and stretched out his hand. But his train, I could see from the steam in his eyes, was not going to stop. The train was, by now, all upon him, and I thought he was about to step back and return to his chair, but instead he cried 'Jump!' and his train, shocked, hurtled to a standstill. Painter's body sank, collapsed, folded neatly, as if he knelt to beg, the sheen on the upturned heels of his shoes kissing the light.

'Not again!' sighed Porlock. He left his fingernails and moved towards Painter. The planet on the floor. Together, Porlock and the rentman began to lift him.

'I will permit,' said Mr Tal, 'my Christian Baudelaire to be borne aloft by Jewish angels.'

Porlock and the rentman, Painter in their grip, neared his chair.

'But arrangements,' said Mr Tal, 'are already in hand to let him fall, as if by accident, just before his entrance into glory.'

'Don't talk to me about arrangements,' said the rentman. Nevertheless, he and Porlock dropped Painter, as if by accident. Dropped, he was, on his arse. Within inches of the glory of the upright chair.

'God!' roared Painter as he fell.

'An inch short of the Promised Land,' observed Porlock.

'What's good enough for Moses –,' began the rentman, who quickly orbited Painter before attempting to restore the giant to his chair.

'Bugger Moses,' said Painter, 'The train, did it stop?'

'Yes,' said the rentman, heaving, desperately heaving. 'Well, to be exact,' he added, 'it crashed, screaming to an almighty and catastrophic halt.' He nudged his glasses.

'Bringing with it,' said Porlock, 'the whole of Heaven, the whole sorry Carnival, just back from the Panto in London – Derek Henderson, chief among them.'

'And, Johanna?' said Painter, now back on his chair.

'I beg your pardon?' said Porlock.

'Johanna,' said Painter, '– she said *she*'d be here.' He did not look up.

'No, *not Johanna*,' said a figure at the hallway door. Romeo.

'Dead?' asked Painter. He did not look up.

'Who? You?' said Romeo, 'No, you're not dead. Not quite.'

'*Johanna*,' said Painter. He did not look up. 'Was *she* dead?' He, Mr Painter, he of all people, should be told.

'No,' said Romeo, the girl had merely been taken away – to a Remand Home, Approved School or perhaps a Nunnery. 'She had,' he said, 'told too many stories.'

*West Herts and Watford Observer*
November 13, 1953

A sixteen-year old girl appeared before Watford Juvenile Court; she was said to make up fantastic tales of where she had been and what she was doing. She was also said to associate with men who carried razors. Her father collapsed in court and her mother said she found her daughter to be pregnant.

'The shop for stories,' said Romeo, 'is closed. No more stories. None.' Romeo looked at Mr Tal. 'The hollow house,' said Romeo, 'is at last surrounded. We, all of us, have come for The Imposter.'

'Ah,' said Porlock, '– as in my Recitation.' He lit a cigarette. 'This,' he said, 'must be when the People call upon the dwarfish Professor to lead them to shining revolution.' Porlock exhaled, and resumed, saying, 'However, in the end, in the press of the crowd, the chaos of the hour, the trick of the night, the glare of the circus –'

'Yes, yes?' said the rentman.

'He, the bleeding dwarf, is shot – *dead*,' concluded Porlock, 'killed by a kind assassin's sudden bullet.'

Only now did I notice that Romeo held in his right hand a tiny plastic pistol, a pistol I'd seen just once before. He was raising it slowly into line with his plastic eye.

'In the July revolution,' said Mr Tal, spotting the pistol, 'on the first evening of fighting the clocks were fired on.'

'Not the clowns?' said Romeo.

Mr Tal shook his head. 'The *clocks*,' he said, 'the *clocks* were fired on.'

Romeo smiled, a molten smile, and fired three chocolate bullets at the straightforward clock on the wall. Then, as the clock exploded into tears, Romeo spun around and fired at Mr Tal. His paper body flew backwards, arms lifted in hilarious surrender, and his custard eyes were wide with it all as he fell to the toppled floor.

'Quick,' said Porlock, 'Before the vagabond dies let us be sure he remembers to mention who precisely he is.'

'Right!' said the rentman.

'But don't allow the bastard to die quoting,' added Porlock.

'It has happened before,' said the rentman.

'Jesus Christ,' said Painter.

'For example,' added the rentman.

'Quite,' said Porlock. 'So, let us hasten to ask the finally dying man who he might finally be.'

'Mr. Clumsy,' said Mr Tal, 'Mr. Clumsy the hunchback.'

'Would the dwarf still be quoting?' said the rentman.

'Mr. Clumsy the hunchback,' said Mr Tal.

'He *is*, you know,' said the rentman.

'Mr. Clumsy the hunchback,' said Mr Tal.

'And so he continues,' said Porlock.

'Mr. Clumsy the hunchback,' said Mr Tal.

'But what –,' I said, 'what *about* the hunchback?'

'This little man,' said Mr Tal, 'this little man' (his voice was cracking like a radio) 'this little man will disappear.'

'Disappear?' I said.

Mr Tal nodded.

'He will disappear,' he said, 'with the coming of the Messiah.'

'Then don't go!' I cried. 'The hunchback must stay. He must, he must. Damn the Messiah!'

Pause. Pause. Pause.

I knelt down and held on to Mr Tal. I held him by the edges, held him and held him, like the dwarf I was, until it dawned that he had long gone – disappeared, vanished, escaped, pissed off, skedaddled, limped speedily away, waddled, like Charlie Chaplin or that Dick Whittington, off back to bloody London. I'm sorry, I will swear, I will; it's just that it's too quiet here, see, or at least it is when it rains and I curse. Mind you, the rest of the time it's too noisy, worse than the East End, it is. I mean, something always goes wrong around here, something wrong with the arrangements. A slight adjustment, and it all goes wrong. Or right. So, am I happy? What me? Here in Heaven? Pushing an empty pram through the snow and burning shoes? Well, I suppose it's what you make of it. I'm more *bored* than anything. Bored every second, every second that goes by, what with nothing to do, on and on.

Nothing to do but clean that mattress and weep, or open the door to whoever it is now. Gasman, rentman, milkman, coalman, doctor, bastard, burning child, wooden monkey, Jehovah. Or, one of his Witnesses. Anyway, some day I will do more. Do something, something or other. But, am I happy? With the arrangements? Well, what do you think? What does anyone think? What does *he* think? Not the one that drowned, the bastard. No, and not *him* either. Not *him*. . . . No, and not that one with the razors, thin as a stick of bloody rhubarb. Disappeared, he did. Got involved with another woman. No, I mean the one with the wings, and the staring mouth, and open eyes, Theology, the holy-demon, the one from the haunted house, Oedipus, him that got the hell out of here, too good for Heaven, he said, Storm, he said, Progress, he said, his Education, he said, his catastrophic Education, he said, as he left me, for the future, me, his *Angela Nova*, he had said, his girl in silk, he had said, his agent of energy, he had said. More like his borrowed Madonna. It was all he wanted. And then he left me, he did, in the woods, with the trees. After the storm, it was, the storm of bloody forgiveness. What does *he* think? What does *he* think? Think of the empty pram?

Pause.

At the end of *The Imposter*, following the reported, off-stage assassination of the Little Professor, all that is left on stage is his suit-case. Enter, stage-right, the son of the Little Professor. The house is still surrounded by both supporters and enemies as well as all the cameras of the press. The son takes up the case and exits through a door that leads to blinding light.

**THE END**

# POST-FACE

## AN OFFICIAL HERTFORDSHIRE COUNTY COUNCIL REPORT (2007)

The Oxhey estate is the main hotspot within the County for deliberate fires and, as a result, also for secondary fires (57 against an average of 9 for the County). The estate is also a hotspot for both fixed and permanent exclusions and for school absenteeism. In terms of crime, Oxhey has an average of 72 crimes per 1000 population, with the highest levels of violent crime, vehicle crime, criminal damage and drug crime in the District. The estate features as highly deprived against measures of Income deprivation, Employment deprivation, Health deprivation and disability, Education skills and training deprivation.

# NOTES

Rather than encumbering the text with endnotes for every quotation used, I have left off all endnote indicators; instead here I provide a detailed set of references, in the order that they appear in my text. All the Walter Benjamin quotations are verbatim, except in the sense that, for novelistic effect, I have very often elided words and not indicated those elisions with the usual three periods. I have sometimes adapted slightly the wording of the newspaper extracts and local testimonies, although never in such a way as to alter the substantive meaning.

## LEFT BEHIND

In September 1939.... See *The Correspondence of Walter Benjamin and Gershom Scholem 1932–1940*, trans. Gary Smith and Andre Lefebvre (Cambridge, MA: Harvard University Press, 1989) pp. 242, 263. n. 1.

a small case... See Momme Brodersesn, *Walter Benjamin A Biography*, tr. Malcolm Green and Ingrida Ligers (London: Verso, 1997) p. 260.

We who have died ... Michael W. Jennings, Howard Eiland and Gary Smith (eds), *Walter Benjamin: Selected Writings*, 4 vols (Cambridge, MA: Harvard University Press, 1996–2003) 1.12.

## SCENE ONE – THE GATE

For the Jews.... Walter Benjamin, *Illuminations*, tr. Harry Zohn (London: Fontana, 1973) p. 255.

Unpacking my library.... Ibid., p. 61.

*West Herts and Watford Observer*, June 29, 1951.

*West Herts and Watford Observer*, July 6, 1951.

These Londoners.... *Illuminations*, p. 163.
The solution.... *Selected Writings*, 2.1.139.
*West Herts and Watford Observer*, July 6, 1951.
I am standing.... *Illuminations*, p. 140.
*West Herts and Watford Observer*, July 27 ,1951.
Knickknacks.... Ursula Marx et al. (eds), *Walter Benjamin's Archive: Images, Texts, Signs*, tr. Esther Leslie (London: Verso, 2007) p. 268.
Palm tree.... Ibid., p. 257.
Electronic television... *Selected Writings*, 2.1.108.
The arrangement... Walter Benjamin, *One Way Street and Other Writings*, tr. Edward Jephcott and Kingsley Shorter (London: Verso, 1979) p. 48.
The whore called.... *Illuminations*, p. 254.
Tiny glass snow-globe.... Benjamin was fascinated by snow-globes – see Theodor Adorno, *Prisms*, tr. Samuel and Shierry Weber (Cambridge, MA: MIT Press, 1983) p. 233.
Science sees... *Selected Writings*, 2.2.474.
The Messiah.... *Illuminations*, p. 130.
*West Herts and Watford Observer*, July 6, 1951.
In the re-purified.... *Selected Writings*, 1.230.
*West Herts and Watford Observer*, July 27, 1951.
There is no telling.... Benjamin, *Illuminations*, p. 199.
The angel would .... Ibid., p. 249.
One of the most remarkable.... *Theodor Adorno and Walter Benjamin, The Complete Correspondence 1928–1940*, ed. Henri Lonitz, tr. Nicholas Walker (Cambridge, MA: Harvard University Press, 1999) p. 132.

## SCENE TWO – THE HOUSE

This glass has been stolen.... This is true.
Yes there was some.... Rose McNamara-Wright, *A Giant on their Doorstep* (nd) p. 11.
The Dick Whittington Pub was opened in 1954, with the name being selected by locals – see *West Herts and Watford Observer*, July 30, 1954.
*Estate News*, August–September 1949, in Local Studies Archive, South Oxhey Library, South Oxhey.

Just jacked it in.... 'By the end of 1958, altogether 1,831 tenants had left South Oxhey, that is some 30 per cent of all the tenants who been housed there since the establishment of the estate' – Margot Jeffreys, 'Londoners in Hertfordshire: The South Oxhey Estate,' in Ruth Glass et al., *London: Aspects of Change* (London: Maggibbon and Kee, 1964) p. 234.

Report of Hertfordshire County Council Education Committee, 1951, quoted in Lloyd Rodwin, *The British New Towns Policy* (Cambridge, MA: Harvard University Press, 1956) p. 134.

It was so quiet.... McNamara-Wright, p. 12.

Firewood.... On January 13, 1951 Mr. Leslie Earl Newell was fined £2 plus £1.1s. costs for committing damage to tree; Mr Newell claimed that his wife was ill and that they had run short of fuel – see *West Herts and Watford Observer*, February 23, 1951.

Because so many.... See, for example, H. G. Maule, 'Social and Psychological Aspects of Re-Housing,' *The Advancement of Science* 13 (1956), 452–76; H. F. Brotherstone and S. P. W. Chave with A. Clewyn-Davies, A. S. Hunter, D. A. Lindsay, A. Scott, C. B. Thomas and E. J. Trimmer, 'General Practice on a New Housing Estate,' *British Journal of Preventive and Social Medicine* 10 (1956), 200–7; F. Barasi and Ann Cartwright, 'The Use of a Questionnaire to Parents at School Medical Examinations,' *The Medical Officer* 98 (1957) 63–5; F. M. Martin, J. H. F. Brotherston and S. P. W. Chave, 'Incidence of Neurosis on a New Housing Estate,' *British Journal of Preventive and Social Medicine* 11 (1957), 199–210; Ann Cartwright, 'The Families and Individuals Who Did Not Cooperate on a Sample Survey,' *The Milbank Memorial Fund Quarterly* 37 (1959), 347–68; Ann Cartwright, 'Some Problems in the Collection and Analysis of Morbidity Data Obtained from Sample Surveys,' *The Milbank Memorial Fund Quarterly* 37 (1959), 33–48.

The touring medical expert.... *Selected Writings*, 2.1.137.

General Practice.... Brotherstone et al.

Forty-five per cent.... Ibid., p. 202.

Backache. Breathlessness.... One or two of these afflictions are imported from other medical studies of the estate:

'personality disorders' comes from Martin et al., p. 199; 'running ears' comes from Cartwright, 'Some Problems', p. 36.

Summoned or.... *One Way Street*, p. 90.

At midnight.... Ibid., p. 61.

The person who.... Cartwright, 'The Families', p. 348.

Why are people.... Ibid., p. 351.

Those who gave.... Ibid., p. 362.

Even the dead.... *Illuminations*, p. 247.

Was it not noticeable.... Ibid., p. 84.

a flattened old man.... This is true; I still have the crucifix.

In a dream.... *One Way Street*, p. 91.

The angel of history.... *Illuminations*, p. 249.

To quote the men.... See Genesis 19.8 where the men of Sodom desire the two angels who are with Lot.

*West Herts and Watford Observer*, November 21, 1952.

This storm propels.... Benjamin, *Illuminations*, p. 249.

*Dispersal*.... See Andrew Saint, 'Spread the People: The LCC's Dispersal Policy, 1889–1965' in Andrew Saint (ed.), *Politics and the People of London* (London: Hambledon Press, 1989).

The Export of Populace.... See J. H. Forshaw and P. Abercrombie, *County of London Plan* (London: Macmillan and Co., 1943) p. 12.

Spontaneous Mass Decentralisation.... Ibid., p. 12.

Storm from paradise.... *Illuminations*, p. 249.

Overspill.... 'London thought it spilled people; there is no spillage with God, He collects'—Rev Douglas W. Thompson, Minister of Carpenders Park and South Methodist Church, 1948–53, quoted in *The Golden Anniversary of Carpender's Park and South Oxhey Methodist Church* (2003) p. 3.

*West Herts and Watford Observer*, April 8, 1949.

Little Moscow.... See *West Herts and Watford Observer*, June 20, 1952.

It was in the very early.... Maule, p. 452. Note that the Community Association was said to be 'agitating for a clinic on the estate...' – *West Herts and Watford Observer*, September 23, 1949.

I have met a woman.... *The Correspondence of Walter Benjamin and Gershom Scholem 1932–1940*, tr. Gary Smith and Andre Lefebvre (Cambridge, MA: Harvard University Press 1992) pp. 72–3.

A painting named.... *Illuminations*, p. 249.

The only person.... *Benjamin and Scholem*, p. 77.

## SCENE THREE – TWO FILMS ARE BRIEFLY PROJECTED

Frederick Lack, James Burnham and Robert Hooper, dirs., *Came The Day (1957)*, Three Rivers Museum of Local History, Rickmansworth.

What we will see.... *Selected Writings,* 2.1.310.

The marching-band is, I believe, an American Forces band, probably from the NATO Headquarters, which is located at nearby Northwood.

The quest for happiness.... *One Way Street*, p. 155.

I had quietly turned.... *Selected Writings*, 3.25.

Walter Ruttmann, dir., *Berlin: Symphony of a Great City* (1927). Ruttman's famous film was a model for Walter Benjamin in his own attempt to represent the city of Berlin – see Esther Leslie, *Walter Benjamin* (London: Reaktion, 2008) p. 28. For details of the showing of this film in Watford see *West Herts and Watford Observer*, February 16, 1951.

People are taught.... *One Way Street*, p. 89.

Berlin is a deserted.... Ibid., p. 178.

To interrupt the world.... *Selected Writings*, 4.170.

Joshua?.... See Joshua 10.12-13: 'And the sun stood still ... until the people had avenged themselves upon their enemies.'

When Walter Benjamin died.... See Ingrid and Konrad Scheurmann, *For Walter Benjamin - Documentation, Essays and a Sketch including: New Documents on Walter Benjamin's Death*, tr. Timothy Nevill (Bonn: AsKI, 1993) pp. 266–8.

You shall now.... *Theodor Adorno and Walter Benjamin*, p. 49.

O. E. Tal.... Ibid., p. 140.

## SCENE FOUR – THE FRONT ROOM

National Corset Week.... *See West Herts and Watford Observer, March 13, 1953.*

*West Herts and Watford Observer*, August 20, 1954.

Perhaps the Holy Ghost.... *Benjamin and Scholem*, p. 190.

For photograph of hotel bill, see Scheurmann, pp. 290–1.

Every hour the telephone.... Walter Benjamin, *Berlin Childhood Around 1900*, tr. Howard Eiland (Cambridge, MA: Harvard University Press, 2006) p. 48.

These Londoners have.... *Selected Writings*, 3.3.

Cinema tickets.... Benjamin wrote in a miniscule hand on any kind of paper he could find; for a series of wonderful photographs of these texts, see *Walter Benjamin's Archive.*

Theodor and Gretel.... *Adorno and Benjamin*, p. 211.

We who have died.... *Selected Writings*, 1.12.

When you are taken.... *One Way Street*, p. 98.

*West Herts and Watford Observer*, April 3, 1953.

The medium obeys.... *Berlin Childhood*, p. 50.

There is.... *Selected Writings*, 4.171.

We were all so young.... McNamara-Wright, p. 53.

The Use of a Questionnaire.... The correct title is 'The Use of a Questionnaire to Parents at School Medical Examinations,' but the schools in question were in South Oxhey.

Have any of the following.... Barasi and Cartwight, p. 65.

*West Herts and Watford Observer*, September 17, 1954.

Isaac Walton's Invincible Specials.... See *West Herts and Watford Observer*, June 11, 1954.

*West Herts and Watford Observer*, August 21, 1953.

The child behind.... *Berlin Childhood*, p. 99.

Susan Jackman.... Author's own memory.

There used to be.... *Illuminations*, p. 93.

On this sofa.... *One Way Street*, p. 49.

Captain Blackwell.... For details of the compulsory purchase of the Blackwell Estates, see LCC records held at London Metropolitan Archives – in particular: LCC/CL/HSG/2/039.

Our *coming.... Illuminations*, p. 246.

We have been.... Ibid., p. 246.
*West Herts and Watford Observer*, December 12, 1954.
My father was.... Sorrel Nunn, letter to the author, 2008.
Even in times.... *Illuminations*, p. 72.
We who have.... *Selected Writings*, 1.12.
Interesting things with lampshades.... Clarendon School Governors' Meetings Minutes, HEd1/177/1, Hertfordshire Archives and Local Studies, Hertford.
*West Herts and Watford Observer*, November 7, 1954.

## SCENE FIVE – STILL THE FRONT ROOM

Among the failings.... *West Herts and Watford Observer*, April 16, 1953.
Frank Harvey.... See *The Poltergeist. A Play in Three Acts* (London: H. F. W. Dean and Sons, 1947).
If only we could get back to London.... Ibid., p. 9.
Like the last train.... Ibid., p. 57.
The extremes encompassed.... *Selected Writings*, 4.185.
One Vincent Ebury, member.... Harvey, p. 22.
Hunting the bogies.... Ibid., p. 29.
Catching sunbeams.... Ibid., p. 29.
School of exile.... *Selected Writings*, 4.136.
Just a man.... Harvey, p. 61.
Ah yes, but.... Ibid., p. 11.
We used, back.... Joan Kennedy, letter to author, July 2008.
Heaven in Hertfordshire.... Leslie Thomas, *Tropic of Ruislip* (London: Pan, 1979) p. 54.
Someone kneels.... *One Way Street*, p. 171.
You know, he does.... Harvey, p. 62.
Rain-Fall Run-Off.... Document dated 23.9.1952, see LCC/CL/HSG/2/39.
the laws of physics.... Harvey, p. 62.
The main thing.... *Selected Writings*, 3.7.
It seems relevant here.... Cartwright, 'Some Problems,' p. 37.
The Agent of energy.... Harvey, p. 34.
Had she touched me.... *One Way Street*, p. 69.
Romeo's last sigh.... *Berlin Childhood*, p. 43.

## SCENE SIX – THE GARDEN IN THE EVENING

Stanley Gale, *Modern Housing Estates: a Practical Guide to their Planning Design and Development for the Use of Town Planners, Architects, Surveyors, Engineers, Municipal Officials, Builders and Others Interested in the Technical and Legal Aspects of the Subject* (London: B. T. Batsford, 1949) p. 272.

The landscape sends.... *Selected Writings*, p. 13.

She is the Madonna.... *One Way Street*, p. 192.

Over 600 quotations.... *Illuminations*, p. 51.

Greetings from Mr Clumsy.... *Berlin Childhood,* p. 121.

Last night Brecht.... *Selected Writings*, 3.338.

In this utopian Europe.... *Selected Writings*, 2.2.749.

I recall a family.... David Reidy, letter to author, July 2008.

He who seeks.... *One Way Street*, p. 314.

No less indispensible.... Ibid., p. 314.

*West Herts and Watford Observer*, June 25, 1950.

The reliability of English.... *Adorno and Benjamin*, p. 34.

The trembling treetops.... *Selected Writings*, 1.13.

Johnny Homeless.... *Selected Writings*, 4.135.

The child becomes.... *Berlin Childhood*, p. 99.

*West Herts and Watford Observer*, June 19, 1953.

Free of the chimes.... *One Way Street*, p. 204.

I remember, before.... *The Golden Anniversary of Carpender's Park and South Oxhey Methodist Church, 1953–2003*, p. 12.

Proust devoting all.... *Illuminations*, p. 198.

*West Herts and Watford Observer*, May 11, 1951.

The Vienna gas board.... *The Correspondence of Walter Benjamin 1910–1940*, tr. Manfred Jacobson and Evelyn Jacobson (Chicago: University of Chicago Press) p. 609.

The literary precipitate.... *One Way Street*, p. 226.

Pacing the Euston platform.... http://www.fullbooks.com/The-Second-Thoughts-of-An-Idle-Fellow.html, p. 36.

Arthur Henry Bicknell.... http://www.stanford.edu/~njenkins/archives/07commentary_w_h_auden_-_family_ghosts_website/index.html.

Of those who.... *Selected Writings*, 2.566.

I took a short cut.... Harold Pinter, *The Caretaker* (London: Methuen, 1960) p. 15.

Somewhere, shoes rain.... *One Way Street*, p. 86.

Got onto the.... Pinter, p. 15.

Belsen.... see C. S. Lewis, *Surprised by Joy* (London: Fontana, 1955) p. 27.

*West Herts and Watford Observer*, May 23, 1945.

Why?.... *Selected Writings*, 2.2.418.

I spoke with my brother.... *The Correspondence of Walter Benjamin*, p. 413.

I can count.... *The Correspondence of Walter Benjamin*, p. 508.

An old man.... *Benjamin and Scholem*, p. 95.

Historical man.... *Selected Writings*, 2.2.542.

I pick it up.... *One Way Street*, p. 337.

*West Herts and Watford Observer*, April 16, 1954.

Why?.... *Selected Writings*, 2.2.418.

Why the world?.... *Berlin Childhood*, p. 117.

Hitler.... *Benjamin and Scholem*, p. 259.

Most of us.... McNamara-Wright, p. 9.

For my dear Stefan.... *One Way Street*, p. 293.

Our child.... *Selected Writings*, 2.2.664.

In September 1939.... see Ester Leslie, *Walter Benjamin* (London: Reaktion, 2007) p. 191 and *Benjamin and Scholem*, p. 263, n. 1.

Has your child.... Barasi and Cartwright, pp. 63–5.

That demonic fellow.... *Selected Writings*, 3.27.

On the Oxhey estate.... John Newsome, *A Hertfordshire Educationist* (Hatfield: University of Hertfordshire Press, 2005) p. 193.

I lie in bed.... *Selected Writings*, 2.2.674.

LIBRARY and SCIENTIFIC BOOK.... see *A Directory of Dealers in Secondhand and Antiquarian Books in the British Isles, 1964–1966* (London: Sheppard Press, 1965). I am grateful to Christoff Mans of Protea Book House, Pretoria and Marianne Harwood of the Antiquarian Booksellers Association, London for locating this entry.

I have hardly been.... *Benjamin and Scholem*, p. 82.

There is no telephone.... *Berlin Childhood*, p. 108.

I could probably make.... *Adorno and Walter Benjamin*, p. 222.
*West Herts and Watford Observer*, November 21, 1952.

## SCENE SEVEN – STILL THE GARDEN IN THE EVENING

*West Herts and Watford Observer*, November 13, 1953.
The whore called.... *Illuminations*, p. 254.
Someone must be.... *Illuminations*, p. 142.
The only way.... *One Way Street*, p. 77.
It is impotence.... *Selected Writings*, 4.167.
Erotic motives.... *The Correspondence of Walter Benjamin*, p. 604.
Books and harlots.... *One Way Street*, p. 69.
I congratulate myself.... *Correspondence of Benjamin and Scholem*, p. 52.
From the library.... *The Correspondence of Walter Benjamin*, p. 243.
Insatiable.... See *West Herts and Watford Observer*, October 13, 1951 where, in relation to the mobile library that then served the Estate, a Mr Lawrence Allaker remarks upon 'the residents' insatiable thirst for books.'
*West Herts and Watford Observer*, January 19, 1950.
*The Estate News*, December 1949.
The Bibliothèque Nationale.... *Adorno and Benjamin*, p. 276.
It has been reported.... Minutes of the Hertfordshire County Council Library Committee, August 24, 1965, HCC 210/2.
*West Herts and Watford Observer*, September 17, 1954.
*Estate News*, August 1949.
*Minutes of the Hertfordshire Workers Education Association*, May 1958, HCC1/177.
The work of W. H. Auden.... Maurice Carpenter, 'Rebel in the Thirties,' unpublished Ms., British Library, X902/5040.
the incorrigible Maurice Carpenter.... Very little has been recorded of Carpenter's life; the best published resources are: Robert Fraser's biography of Carpenter's better-known friend, the poet George Barker – see Robert Fraser,

*The Chameleon Poet* (London: Jonathan Cape, 2001) and Andy Croft, *A Life of Randall Swingler* (Manchester: Manchester UP, 2003).

I Maurice Carpenter.... Please note that every line that Porlock utters in, or as, the character of Carpenter is either a direct quotation from Carpenter or, just occasionally, a very slight adaptation.

Edith Sitwell.... See Richard Greene (ed.), *Selected Letters of Edith Sitwell* (London: Virago, 1997) pp. 351–2.

My alter ego.... See Carpenter, *Rebel*, p. 1.

Moscow Dynamo FC.... Dynamo toured England in 1945, and their games were closely followed by *The Daily Worker* – see Ronald Kowalski and Dilwyn Porter, 'Mysterious Muscovites: Moscow Dynamo's British Tour, 1945,' *History Review* 33 (1999) 9–11.

I was, you must.... See Carpenter, *Rebel*, p. 14.

a bathing beauty in Leningrad.... The *Daily Worker* did, indeed, feature such a photograph – see *Daily Worker*, May 10, 1948.

In the Dirty Thirties.... See Carpenter, *Rebel*, pp. 30–2.

But what I really wanted.... Ibid., p. 32.

Mary Rose.... Ibid., p. 129.

An outstanding female Communist.... Benjamin quoted in Brodersen, p. 137.

Where are you England?.... 'The Ballad of John Nameless' in Maurice Carpenter, Jack Lindsay and Honor Arundel (eds), *New Lyrical Ballads* (London: Nicolson and Watson, 1945) pp. 119–30.

We are midwives.... 'Machine Stops: Night Shift,' ibid., p. 59.

The trouble in the street.... Maurice Carpenter, *The Tall Interpreter* (London: Meridian Books, 1948) p. 12.

All good poets.... Maurice Carpenter, *The Indifferent Horseman: The Divine Comedy of Samuel Taylor Coleridge* (London: Elek Books, 1954) p. 199.

The time he lived.... Ibid., p. 199.

Like K. in *The Trial*, Ibid., p. 199.

The singer.... Carpenter, *Tall Interpreter*, p. 6.

I once saw.... Neil Hamilton, interview with the author, 2008.

Your writhing.... Carpenter, *Tall Interpreter*, p. 38.

I failed.... Carpenter, *Rebel*, p. 97.
*Her Majesty's Inspectors' Survey of Adult Education* (1954), HEd1/177/1.
The masses.... *Selected Writings*, 2.1.136.
Brecht found me.... *Selected Writings*, 3.338.
*Estate News*, May 1949.
I am close.... *Selected Writings*, 2.1.63.
A welter of abortions.... *The Correspondence of Walter Benjamin*, p. 542.
The comic figure.... *Selected Writings*, 2.2.590.
The clowning.... Ibid., 2.2.426.
If one had to.... *One Way Street*, p. 103.
The big event.... Vanessa Sparrowhawk, letter to author, January 2009.
I was born.... *Selected Writings*, 2.2.713.
The star.... Ibid., 2.2.713.
*West Herts and Watford Observer*, April 20, 1951.
Humanity is born.... *Selected Writings*, 2.1305.
Walter Benjamin's death.... Hannah Arendt, Introduction to *Illuminations*, pp. 11, 24.
Irony.... *Selected Writings*, 2.2.704.
If you knew.... *Correspondence of Benjamin and Scholem*, p. 77.
I have hardly.... Ibid., p. 82.
Dora has opened.... Ibid., p. 242.
Soon after.... See Martin Jay and Gary Smith,'A Talk with Mona Jean Benjamin, Kim Yvon Benjamin and Michael Benjamin,' *Benjamin Studien/Studies* 1 (2002) 11–25.
The house.... *Berlin Childhood*, p. 102.
The proletariat.... *One Way Street*, p. 183.
For my dear Stefan.... Ibid., p. 293.
If you knew.... *Correspondence of Benjamin and Scholem*, p. 77.
It is impotence.... *Selected Writings*, 4.167.

## SCENE EIGHT – THE GARDEN, NOW FROZEN, AT NIGHT

You have.... *Selected Writings*, 2.1.86.
Everyone on the estate.... The author's own memory.

The Metaphysics of Youth.... *Selected Writings*, 1.6–17
Our glances meet.... Ibid., p. 16.
The dance now begins.... Ibid., p. 16.
We do not arouse.... Ibid., p. 16.
Most people supported.... The author's own memory.
Our bodies make.... *Selected Writings*, 1.16.
How we love.... Ibid., 1.16.
We are in a house.... Ibid., 1.16–17.
We hurl ourselves.... Ibid., 1.16.
Never was a night.... Ibid., 1.16.
Our hands slide.... Ibid., 1.16.
The thinker.... Ibid., 2.1.216.
In Paris.... Quoted in Brodersen, p. 244.
We stand.... *Selected Writings*, 1.16.
Our fleeing soul.... Ibid., 1.16.
She walks.... Ibid., 1.16.
*Estate News*, January 1950.
Her stately step.... *Selected Writings*, 1.16
Where people.... Ibid., 1.16.
When did night.... Ibid., 1.16.
*West Herts and Watford Observer*, January 23, 1948.
The music.... *Selected Writings*, 1.16.
And to the.... *Berlin Childhood*, p. 119.
But we *know*.... *Selected Writings*, 1.17.
The poets.... Ibid., 1.17.
And the saints.... Ibid., 1.17.
The house surrounded.... Ibid., 2.2.579.
A situation with.... *The Correspondence of Walter Benjamin*, p. 342.
These Londoners.... *Selected Writings*, 3.3.
A lover.... *Berlin Childhood*, p. 128.
Unmasking.... *Selected Writings*, 2.1.306.
There are spies.... *Benjamin and Scholem*, p. 47.
Do you not.... *The Correspondence of Walter Benjamin*, p. 351.
Because my father.... Sorrel Nunn, letter to author, March 2009.
Dear Invisible Listeners.... *Selected Writings*, 2.1.250.
The policemen.... Ibid., 1.17.

ITMA, the BBC radio comedy – see http://www.bbc.co.uk/liverpool/localhistory/journey/stars/tommy_handley/itma.shtml.

I don't mind if I do.... This was the catchphrase of Colonel Humphrey Chinstrap, the dipsomaniac ITMA character, who, with these words, would turn almost any remark into the offer of a drink.

Truth.... *One Way Street*, p. 95.

In September 1945.... See Charles Stuart (ed.), *The Reith Diaries* (London: Collins, 1975) p. 352.

It is a fact.... See Jeffrey Mehlman, *Walter Benjamin for Children: An Essay on his Radio Years* (Chicago: Chicago University Press, 1993) p. 1.

I feel like a chemist.... *Selected Writings*, 2.2.536.

My weights.... Ibid., 2.2.537.

It should be here noted.... See, for example, Leslie, p. 215.

Radio.... *Benjamin and Scholem*, p. 130.

This brings me.... *Selected Writings*, 2.2.540.

The radio listener.... Ibid., 2.2.544.

No reader.... Ibid., 2.2.544.

The headmaster.... The author's own memory.

An infant prodigy.... *Selected Writings*, 2.1.309.

Fish and Chips.... *The Estate News*, December–January 1949–50.

J. O. Knight.... Ibid.

And what do I.... *Berlin Childhood*, p. 132.

*West Herts and Watford Observer*, December 4, 1953.

For many of us.... Maud Atkinson, letter to the author, March 2008.

*Minutes*.... HCC 204/3.

The damp boredom.... *One Way Street*, p. 225.

When yawning.... *Selected Writings*, 4.184.

People who.... *Selected Writings*, 2.2.658.

We penetrate.... *One Way Street*, p. 237.

A few dozen.... Ibid., p. 96.

For the Jews.... *Illuminations*, p. 255.

*Estate News*, October 1950.

In the typist's.... *Selected Writings*, 2.1.309.

*Her Majesty's*.... HEd1/177/1.

For years I.... Ray Breeze, interview with the author, January 2009.
Bedtime has come.... *Berlin Childhood*, p. 100.
Four times.... See Martin et al., pp. 158–61.
In the early days.... Joan Manning, interview with author, June 2008.
Telepathic girl.... *Selected Writings*, 2.1.210.
I'd like to.... *Benjamin and Scholem*, p. 227.
Nocturnal thoughts.... *Selected Writings*, 2.2.424.
Suicides.... Ibid., 2.1.15.
*West Herts and Watford Observer*, April 16, 1953.

## SCENE NINE – STILL THE FROSTED GARDEN AT NIGHT

The great authentic.... *Selected Writings*, 1.230.
Only now.... Ibid., 1.230.
You sleepily.... Ibid., 2.1.360.
I have hardly.... Ibid., 2.1.851.
Human multitudes.... *One Way Street*, p. 103.
Great cities.... Ibid., p. 59.
Under the open.... *Illuminations*, p. 84.
It was.... David Reidy and Joan Kennedy, letters to the author, May 2009.
A breath of ice.... *Benjamin and Scholem*, p. 205.
I remember.... June Moore, David Reidy, Joan Manning.
My husband.... Name withheld.
The local Spanish.... See Scheurmann, p. 270.
Medieval Scholastics.... *Selected Writings*, 2.1.50.
Christian in the.... *The Correspondence of Walter Benjamin*, p. 552.
Violent migraines.... *Selected Writings*, 3.52.
Under the open.... *Illuminations*, p. 84.
In the war.... Sorrel Nun, letter to the author.
Utopia.... *Selected Writings*, 3.134.
Invariably.... Gale, p. 11.
The weapons.... Forshaw and Abercrombie, p. 124.
This era.... *Illuminations*, p. 141.
Science sees.... *Selected Writings*, 2.2.474.

In everything.... Ibid., 1.16.

*West Herts and Watford Observer*, December 23, 1949.

We Have Bad Dreams.... See Hamlet's words: 'I could...count myself a king of infinite space – were it not that I have bad dreams'– *Hamlet*, II.ii.251–9.

How we safeguard.... *Selected Writings*, 1.16.

*LITTLE MISS MUFFET*.... The drama that here follows is simply a speeded-up version of the actual pantomime text – see G. Champneys Burnham and Conrad Carter, *Little Miss Muffett. A Basic Pantomime in Two Acts* (London: Samuel French Ltd., 1950).

We won't.... Ibid., p. 2.

No *soap?*.... Ibid., p. 3.

Oh whisper.... Ibid., p. 3.

For I have washed.... Ibid., p. 16.

I say.... Ibid., p. 16.

All right.... Ibid., p. 24.

No – the fullness.... Ibid., p. 25.

Lummy.... Ibid., p. 32.

But I'm deaf.... Ibid., p. 30.

So much for.... Ibid., p. 30.

Cookie Cookie!.... Ibid., p. 30.

Hullo children.... Ibid., p. 51.

Oh, Clark Gable.... Ibid., p. 32.

Now, now.... Ibid., p. 39.

For it is.... Ibid., p. 53.

Particularly.... Ibid., p. 54.

Not that I'm one.... Ibid., p. 29 – this astonishing monologue is quoted verbatim.

The English stage.... *Selected Writings*, 2.2.577.

The pantomime of existence.... Ibid., 2.1.134.

Suffering.... Ibid., 2.1.331.

The Messianic.... *One Way Street*, p. 156.

Every carnival.... *Selected Writings*, 3.26.

There is an infinity.... This should, of course, be 'There is an infinity of hope but not for us,' – as quoted by Benjamin, see *Selected Writings*, 2.2.798.

The historian.... *Selected Writings*, 4.405.

What do I hear.... *Berlin Childhood*, p. 132.

The camera.... *Illuminations*, p. 171.
male sexuality.... *Selected Writings*, 4.167.
Why?.... Ibid., 2.2.418.
The Socratic inquiry.... Ibid., 1.53.
Murder.... Ibid., 3.5.
Suicide.... Ibid., 2.1.15.
*Secret Germany*, Ibid., 2.2.466.
Claus von Stauffenberg.... On 20 July 1944, Claus von Stauffenberg placed a suitcase containing a bomb against a table next to Hitler – see Michael Baigent and Richard Leigh, *Secret Germany* (New York: Random House, 2006).
Again and again.... *One Way Street*, p. 100.
The moment.... Ibid., p. 100.
Their entry.... Ibid., p. 100.
Our reading.... Ibid., p. 100.

## SCENE TEN – THE CORONATION AND THE BEAUTIFUL POURING RAIN

I have not.... *The Correspondence of Walter Benjamin*, p. 292.
I have.... *Correspondence of Benjamin and Scholem*, p. 60.
I started.... Ibid., p. 60.
It is.... *The Correspondence of Walter Benjamin*, p. 91.
inability to make.... *One Way Street*, p. 294.
In the very early.... Neil Hamilton, letter to author.
Every morning.... *Selected Writings*, 2.2.729.
And yet.... Ibid., 2.2.279.
It is because.... Ibid., 2.2.279.
Last night.... *Selected Writings*, 3.335.
Women.... Ibid., 3.335.
Even commenting.... Ibid., 3.335.
She exhibits.... *The Correspondence of Walter Benjamin*, p. 296.
Through the beautiful.... Ibid., p. 9.
Constant rain.... Ibid., p. 107.
There is.... Ibid., p. 452.
Nothing can vanish.... *Selected Writings*, 2.1.149.
serenely endured.... *The Correspondence of Walter Benjamin*, p. 21.

*West Herts and Watford Observer*, 5 June 1953.
I was struck.... *Berlin Childhood*, p. 107.
I experience.... *Selected Writings*, 2.1.85.
the assassination.... Ibid., 2.1.85.
Only in extinction.... *Illuminations*, p. 168.
You start.... *Selected Writings*, 2.1.85.
Chiaroscuro.... Ibid., 3.13.
He cannot.... Ibid., 1.443.
The figure.... *Illuminations*, p. 133.
January the 14th.... LCC/CL/HSG/2/039, London Metropolitan Archives.
The beggar.... *Illuminations*, p. 133.
A man.... Ibid., p. 133.
The Queen shall.... See http://www.oremus.org/liturgy/coronation/cor1953b.html.
An actor.... *Illuminations*, p. 148.
She is.... *The Correspondence of Walter Benjamin*, p. 17.
The coffin.... *Selected Writings*, 1.338.
The Queen kneeling.... See http://www.oremus.org/liturgy/coronation/cor1953b.html.
Glass.... *Selected Writings*, 2.2.734.
In the meantime.... See http://www.oremus.org/liturgy/coronation/cor1953b.html.
As I kissed.... *Selected Writings*, 2.2.589.
Mannequin.... *Berlin Childhood*, p. 78.
The moment.... *Selected Writings*, 2.189.
Apollo.... Ibid., 2.1.89.
A Daphne.... *Selected Writings*, 2.2.502.
*The Princes*.... See http://www.oremus.org/liturgy/coronation/cor1953b.html.
Deserted streets.... *One Way Street*, p. 230.
Dreaming.... *Selected Writings*, 2.1.3.
*Then shall*.... See http://www.oremus.org/liturgy/coronation/cor1953b.html.
a full programme.... See *West Herts and Watford Observer*, 5 June 1953.
Storm of forgiveness.... *Selected Writings*, 1.286.
When the Archbishop.... http://www.oremus.org/liturgy/coronation/cor1953b.html.

Forty-nine.... *Selected Writings*, 2.1.841.
It is said.... Ibid., 2.1.223.
A mechanical.... *One Way Street*, p. 87.
This is.... See http://www.oremus.org/liturgy/coronation/cor1953b.html.
Biblical figurines.... *One Way Street*, p. 87.
Drink ye.... See http://www.oremus.org/liturgy/coronation/cor1953b.html.
Do this.... Ibid.
Hoylake Gardens – see *West Herts and Watford Observer*, June 5, 1953.
I look.... http://www.oremus.org/liturgy/coronation/cor1953b.html.
I have fallen.... *Correspondence of Benjamin and Scholem*, p. 148.
*West Herts and Watford Observer*, June 5, 1953.
Then her Majesty.... See http://www.oremus.org/liturgy/coronation/cor1953b.html.
History.... *Selected Writings*, 4.164.
A kaleidoscope.... Ibid., 4.164.
The historical.... Ibid., 4.407.
And the kaleidoscope.... Ibid., 4.164.
Film.... *Illuminations*, p. 229.
So that now.... Ibid., p. 229.

## SCENE ELEVEN – STILL THE CORONATION AND THE BEAUTIFUL POURING RAIN

Foaming-at-the-Mouth.... This is the seaside setting for ITMA.
A barge-pole.... *Selected Writings*, 4.407.
Mr. N. Kemp.... See *West Herts and Watford Observer*, August 20, 1954.
Having arrived.... See Saul David, *Churchill's Sacrifice of the Highland Division* (London: Brassey's, 2004).
One of the last ships.... *The Correspondence of Walter Benjamin*, p. 412.
*West Herts and Watford Observer*, July 6, 1951.

Few, very few.... See Patrick Abercrombie, *Greater London Plan 1944* (London: His Majesty's Stationery Office, 1945) p. 98.

A final ice cream.... *Selected Writings*, 2.2.678.

*Estate News*, August 1950.

Nothing is more.... *Selected Writings*, 2.1.299.

Walter Benjamin had hoped.... See Leslie, p. 206 and Brodersen, p. 252.

I must be.... *One Way Street*, p. 178.

If the sun.... *Selected Writings*, 2.1.107.

Gambling at the seaside.... *Selected Writings*, 2.2.414.

The church.... *One Way Street*, p. 80.

In 1941.... See *Walter Benjamin and Gershom Scholem*, p. 242, n. 11.

We can now.... *Theodor Adorno and Walter Benjamin*, p. 12.

Leaving Europe.... *The Correspondence of Walter Benjamin*, p. 140.

When we first.... Maud Atkinson, letter to the author.

I am pointing.... *The Correspondence of Walter Benjamin*, p. 516.

Such questions.... *Walter Benjamin and Gershom Scholem*, p. 109.

London bus tickets.... *Theodor Adorno and Walter Benjamin*, p. 75.

Cul-de-sacs can often.... Gale, p. 5.

The deathbed.... *Illuminations*, p. 93.

A sequence.... Ibid., p. 93.

The storyteller.... Ibid., p. 93.

If there really.... *Illuminations*, p. 177.

A half-day's.... *The Correspondence of Walter Benjamin*, p. 296.

You must remind.... Ibid., p. 296.

I dreamed.... *Selected Writings*, 3.335–6.

The treads.... Gale, p. 80.

These staircases.... *One Way Street*, p. 338.

With the rises.... Gale, p. 80.

I am now treading.... *The Correspondence of Walter Benjamin*, p. 558.

And the hand-rail.... Gale, p. 80.

A sound rises.... *Selected Writings*, 2.2.665.
These Londoners.... *Selected Writings*, 3.3.
The stairs.... *Selected Writings*, 1.417.
What is enacted.... Ibid., 1.417.
I am unable.... *The Correspondence of Walter Benjamin*, p. 431.

## SCENE TWELVE – REMOVAL

In the early days.... Neil Hamilton, letter to author.
The Thames provides all forms of urban escape.... Abercrombie, p. 84.
By the end of 1958.... Margot Jeffreys, 'Londoners in Hertfordshire,' in Ruth Glass et al., *London: Aspects of Change* (London: MacGibbon and Kee, 1964) p. 234.
Eternal Sunday.... *Berlin Childhood*, p. 47.
Sleeping cars.... *One Way Street*, p. 82.
One Sunday morning.... Marjorie Matthews – a memory of the author's.
Stanley Holloway.... Holloway was an entertainer famous for his comic monologues, or recitations on the radio.
In 1963.... See HEd1/178/1. See Rodolfo Usigli, *The Imposter. A Play for Demagogues*, tr. Ramon Layera (Pittsburgh, PA: Latin American Literary Review Press, 2005).
I dreamed.... *One Way Street*, p. 51.
My Mexican professor.... *The Correspondence of Walter Benjamin*, p. 82.
The exiled professor.... Usigli, p. 59.
The idiot world.... Ibid., pp. 35–6.
And so the people.... Ibid., p. 102.
Lead us.... Ibid., p. 103.
Just let me stay dead! Ibid., p. 105.
The buried man.... *Selected Writings*, 4.165.
One is very glad to be alive.... Walter Benjamin and Gretel Adorno, *Correspondence 1930–1940* (London: Wiley and Sons, 2007) p. 142.
win the energies.... *One Way Street*, p. 236.
We used to call.... McNamara-Wright, p. 56.
*Estate News*, June 1952.

What is truly.... *Selected Writings*, 2.1.206.
A messianic face.... Ibid., 4.403.
We *feel*.... Ibid., 1.103.
The mask.... Ibid., 2.1.222.
Unmasking *others*.... Ibid., 2.1.306.
Only a bad actor.... *Illuminations*, p. 133.
An actor.... *Illuminations*, p. 148.
One lacks.... Walter Benjamin and Gretel Adorno, p. 142.

## SCENE THIRTEEN – THE THRESHOLD OF THE HOTEL

According to.... See Brodersen, pp. 254–6; Scheurmann, p. 268; Carina Birman, *The Narrow Foothold* (London: Hearing Eye, 2006) p. 4.
And so, alone in my room.... Walter Benjamin and Gretel Adorno, p. 289.
A room.... *The Correspondence of Walter Benjamin*, p. 153.
One of the women.... See Birman, p. 5.
A situation.... *Theodor Adorno and Walter Benjamin*, p. 342.
The air.... *Walter Benjamin and Gershom Scholem*, p. 27.
At some point.... See Brodersen, p. 256.
As if dying.... *The Correspondence of Walter Benjamin*, p. 220.
Who was Kafka?.... *Selected Writings*, 2.2.495.
The person.... *Walter Benjamin and Gershom Scholem*, p. 243.
'I am unclear therefore I am Jewish'.... *The Correspondence of Walter Benjamin*, p. 81.
It would be.... *Selected Writings*, 2.2.712.
I am not.... Ibid., 2.1.63.
In Moscow.... *One Way Street*, p. 228.
In these rooms.... Ibid., p. 228.
The most beautiful.... Walter Benjamin and Gretel Adorno, p. 142.
I can hear the sea.... Ibid., p. 296.
Hitler...Chaplin.... *Selected Writings*, 2.2.792.
An elegiac beauty.... Ibid., 2.1.345.
The film ends.... Ibid., 2.1.200.

The wheezing.... *Illuminations*, p. 209.
The hotel owner.... Scheurmann, p. 271.
Flatulence.... *Selected Writings*, 2.2.426.
Telepathic girl.... Ibid., 2.1.210.
Benjamin's possessions.... See Brodersen, p. 260.
What weighs most.... Walter Benjamin and Gretel Adorno, p. 288.
The people.... Ibid., p. 78.
I put my hands.... *Berlin Childhood*, p. 60.
The praying man.... *Selected Writings*, 1.8.
Now for the.... Burnham and Carter, p. 39.
All decisive blows.... *One Way Street*, p. 49.
Mr. Clumsy.... *Berlin Childhood*, pp. 121–2.
If there is pain.... Ibid., p. 164.
If a person.... *One Way Street*, p. 54.
Greetings.... *Berlin Childhood*, p. 121.
Oedipus.... *Selected Writings*, 2.2.579.
Warmth is ebbing.... *One Way Street*, p. 58.
The local.... Scheurmann, p. 97.
The public.... *Selected Writings*, 2.1.145.
The Port Bou register.... See Brodersen, p. 258 and Scheurmann, p. 270.
Walter Benjamin's grave... rental.... See Scheurmann, p. 272.
You think.... *Selected Writings*, 2.1.199.
Walter Benjamin's Catholic grave.... See Scheurmann, p. 273.
One is.... Walter Benjamin and Gretel Adorno, p. 142.
Alive in spite.... Ibid., p. 142.
It is not known.... See Leslie, p. 227.
I have.... *One Way Street*, p. 337.
*As if.... The Correspondence of Walter Benjamin*, p. 34.
That we may.... *Selected Writings*, 2.1.65.
One of them.... Ibid., 3.5.
Murderer.... Ibid., 3.5.
Her decision.... Ibid., 1.336.
Negative replies.... *One Way Street*, p. 190.
Nothing.... Ibid., p. 55.
*But* this state.... Ibid., p. 55.

I lose.... *Berlin Childhood*, p. 72.

Marx says.... *Selected Writings*, 4.402.

But perhaps.... Ibid., 4.402.

Perhaps revolutions.... Ibid., 4.402.

On October 8, 1952.... See John Withington, *The Disastrous History of London* (London: History Press, 2004).

I will permit.... *Theodor Adorno and Walter Benjamin*, p. 317.

But arrangements.... Ibid., p. 317.

*West Herts and Watford Observer*, 13 November 1953.

This must be when.... See Uglisi, p. 118.

In the July.... *Illuminations*, p. 253.

Mr Clumsy.... *Berlin Childhood*, p. 121.

This little man.... *Illuminations*, p. 129.

At the end.... Uglisi, p. 120.

The Oxhey estate.... See www.hertslink.org/hertfordshire forward/content/.../Item6AppB.doc.

# BIBLIOGRAPHY

## WORKS BY WALTER BENJAMIN

*Illuminations*, tr. Harry Zohn (London: Fontana, 1973).

*One Way Street and Other Writings*, tr. Edward Jephcott and Kingsley Shorter (London: Verso, 1979).

*The Correspondence of Walter Benjamin and Gershom Scholem 1932–1940*, tr. Gary Smith and Andre Lefebvre (Cambridge, MA: Harvard University Press, 1989).

*The Correspondence of Walter Benjamin 1910–1940*, tr. Manfred Jacobson and Evelyn Jacobson (Chicago: University of Chicago Press, 1994).

*Walter Benjamin: Selected Writings*, 4 vols, ed. Michael W. Jennings, Howard Eiland and Gary Smith (Cambridge, MA: Harvard University Press, 1996–2003).

*Theodor Adorno and Walter Benjamin, The Complete Correspondence 1928–1940*, ed. Henri Lonitz, tr. Nicholas Walker (Cambridge, MA: Harvard University Press, 1999).

*Berlin Childhood Around 1900*, tr. Howard Eiland (Cambridge, MA: Harvard University Press, 2006).

*On Hashish*, tr. Scott J Thompson (Cambridge, MA: Harvard University Press, 2006).

*Walter Benjamin's Archive: Images, Texts, Signs*, ed. Ursula Marx et al., tr. Esther Leslie (London: Verso, 2007).

*Walter Benjamin and Gretel Adorno, Correspondence 1930–1940*, ed. Henri Lonitz, Christoph Godde and Wieland Hoban (London: Wiley and Sons, 2007).

## LETTERS AND ORAL TESTIMONIES

Maud Atkinson, Margaret Beech, Ray Breeze, Neil Hamilton, Don Jones, Joan Kennedy, John Laver, Joan Manning, June Moore, David Reidy, Alfred Rundle, Vanessa Sparrowhawk and Sorel Nunn.

## UNPUBLISHED MATERIALS

*Estate News* (1948–52), Local Studies Archive, South Oxhey Library, South Oxhey.

Clarendon School Governors' Meetings Minutes (HEd1/177/1), Minutes of the Hertfordshire County Council Library Committee (HCC 210/2), Minutes of the Hertfordshire Workers Education Association, May 1958 (HCC1/177), Her Majesty's Inspectors' Survey of Adult Education, 1954 (HEd1/177/1) – Hertfordshire Archives and Local Studies, Hertford.

Public Inquiry. Blackwell Estates Compulsory Purchase (LCC/CL/HSG/2/039), London Metropolitan Archives.

Maurice Carpenter, Rebel in the Thirties, unpublished Ms., British Library, X902/5040.

## OTHER WORKS REFERENCED

*A Directory of Dealers in Secondhand and Antiquarian Books in the British Isles, 1964–1966.* London: Sheppard Press, 1965.

Abercrombie, P. (1945), *Greater London Plan 1944.* London: His Majesty's Stationery Office.

Adorno, T. (1983), *Prisms*, tr. Samuel and Shierry Weber. Cambridge, MA: MIT Press.

Baigent, M. and R. Leigh (2006), *Secret Germany.* New York: Random House.

Barasi, F. and A. Cartwright (1957), 'The use of a questionnaire to parents at school medical examinations', *The Medical Officer*, 98, 63–5.

Birman, C. (2006), *The Narrow Foothold.* London: Hearing Eye.

Brodersesn, M. (1997), *Walter Benjamin A Biography*, tr. Malcolm Green and Ingrida Ligers. London: Verso.

Brotherstone, H. F. and S. P. W. Chave with A. Clewyn-Davies, A. S. Hunter, D. A. Lindsay, A. Scott, C. B. Thomas and E. J. Trimmer (1956), 'General practice on a new housing estate', *British Journal of Preventive and Social Medicine*, 10, 200–7.

Carpenter, M. (1948), *The Tall Interpreter.* London: Meridian Books.

—(1954), *The Indifferent Horseman: The Divine Comedy of Samuel Taylor Coleridge.* London: Elek Books.

Carpenter, M., J. Lindsay and H. Arundel (eds) (1945), *New Lyrical Ballads.* London: Nicolson and Watson.

Cartwright, A. (1959), 'The families and individuals who did not cooperate on a Sample Survey', *The Milbank Memorial Fund Quarterly*, 37, 347–68.

—(1959), 'Some problems in the collection and analysis of morbidity data obtained from sample surveys', *The Milbank Memorial Fund Quarterly*, 37, 33–48.

Champneys Burnham, G. and C. Carter (1950), *Little Miss Muffett. A Basic Pantomime in Two Acts.* London: Samuel French Ltd.

Croft, A. (2003), *A Life of Randall Swingler.* Manchester: Manchester University Press.

David, S. (2004), *Churchill's Sacrifice of the Highland Division.* London: Brassey's.

Forshaw, J. H. and P. Abercrombie (1943), *County of London Plan.* London: Macmillan and Co.

Fraser, R. (2001), *The Chameleon Poet.* London: Jonathan Cape.

Gale, S. (1949), *Modern Housing Estates: A Practical Guide to Their Planning Design and Development for the Use of Town Planners, Architects, Surveyors, Engineers, Municipal Officials, Builders and Others Interested in the Technical and Legal Aspects of the Subject.* London: B.T. Batsford.

Glass, R. et al. (1964), *London: Aspects of Change.* London: Maggibbon and Kee.

Greene, R. (ed.) (1997), *Selected Letters of Edith Sitwell.* London: Virago.

Harvey, F. (1947), *The Poltergeist. A Play in Three Acts.* London: H.F.W. Dean and Sons.

Jay, M. and G. Smith (2002), 'A talk with Mona Jean Benjamin, Kim Yvon Benjamin and Michael Benjamin', *Benjamin Studien/Studies*, 1, 11–25.

Kowalski, R. and D. Porter (1999), 'Mysterious Muscovites: Moscow Dynamo's British Tour, 1945', *History Review*, 33, 9–11.

Leslie, E. (2007), *Walter Benjamin*. London: Reaktion.

Lewis, C. S. (1955), *Surprised by Joy*. London: Fontana.

Martin, F. M., J. H. F. Brotherston and S. P. W. Chave (1957), 'Incidence of neurosis on a new housing estate', *British Journal of Preventive and Social Medicine*, 11, 199–210.

Maule, H. G. (1956), 'Social and psychological aspects of re-housing', *The Advancement of Science*, 13, 452–76.

McNamara-Wright, R. (n.d.), *A Giant on Their Doorstep*.

Mehlman, J. (1993), *Walter Benjamin for Children: An Essay on His Radio Years*. Chicago, IL: Chicago University Press.

Newsome, J. (2005), *A Hertfordshire Educationist*. Hatfield: University of Hertfordshire Press.

Pinter, H. (1960), *The Caretaker*. London: Methuen.

Rodwin, L. (1956), *The British New Towns Policy*. Cambridge, MA: Harvard University Press.

Saint, A. (ed.) (1989), *Politics and the People of London*. London: Hambledon Press.

Scheurmann, I. and S. Konrad (1993), *For Walter Benjamin, Documentation, Essays and a Sketch Including: New Documents on Walter Benjamin's Death*, tr. Timothy Nevill. Bonn: AsKI.

Stuart, C. (ed.) (1975), *The Reith Diaries*. London: Collins.

Thomas, L. (1979), *Tropic of Ruislip*. London: Pan.

Usigli, R. (2005), *The Imposter. A Play for Demagogues*, tr. Ramon Layera. Pittsburgh, PA: Latin American Literary Review Press.

Withington, J. (2004), *The Disastrous History of London*. London: History Press.

## FILMS

Walter Ruttmann, dir., *Berlin: Symphony of a Great City* (1927).

Frederick Lack, James Burnham and Robert Hooper, dirs., *Came The Day (1957)*, Three Rivers Museum of Local History, Rickmansworth.

# INDEX